T0247631

Considerations Around the Use of Intensive Outpatient Programs for Service Members Who Experienced Sexual Trauma in the U.S. Military

KRISTIE L. GORE, SAMANTHA CHERNEY, SARAH WEILANT,
JUSTIN HUMMER, LINDA COTTRELL, COREEN FARRIS

Prepared for the Defense Health Agency Psychological Health
Center of Excellence
Approved for public release; distribution unlimited

NATIONAL DEFENSE RESEARCH INSTITUTE

For more information on this publication, visit **www.rand.org/t/RRA668-2**.

About RAND

The RAND Corporation is a research organization that develops solutions to public policy challenges to help make communities throughout the world safer and more secure, healthier and more prosperous. RAND is nonprofit, nonpartisan, and committed to the public interest. To learn more about RAND, visit www.rand.org.

Research Integrity

Our mission to help improve policy and decisionmaking through research and analysis is enabled through our core values of quality and objectivity and our unwavering commitment to the highest level of integrity and ethical behavior. To help ensure our research and analysis are rigorous, objective, and nonpartisan, we subject our research publications to a robust and exacting quality-assurance process; avoid both the appearance and reality of financial and other conflicts of interest through staff training, project screening, and a policy of mandatory disclosure; and pursue transparency in our research engagements through our commitment to the open publication of our research findings and recommendations, disclosure of the source of funding of published research, and policies to ensure intellectual independence. For more information, visit www.rand.org/about/research-integrity.

RAND's publications do not necessarily reflect the opinions of its research clients and sponsors.

Published by the RAND Corporation, Santa Monica, Calif.
© 2023 RAND Corporation
RAND® is a registered trademark.

Library of Congress Cataloging-in-Publication Data is available for this publication.

ISBN:978-1-9774-0793-1

Cover: SDI Productions/Getty Images.

Limited Print and Electronic Distribution Rights

About This Report

Section 702 of the fiscal year 2019 National Defense Authorization Act directed the U.S. Department of Defense to conduct a pilot study to assess the feasibility and advisability of using intensive outpatient treatment programs to address posttraumatic stress disorder and associated mental health problems among service members who have experienced sexual harassment or sexual assault while in the military. The Assistant Secretary of Defense for Health Affairs and the Defense Health Agency (DHA) Psychological Health Center of Excellence (PHCoE) commissioned the RAND Corporation's National Defense Research Institute to conduct two studies that supplement PHCoE's efforts to address Section 702's stipulation. The first study is a literature synthesis on treatment effectiveness, barriers and facilitators to treatment, and mental health symptoms associated with sexual harassment and sexual assault in the military, the results of which are detailed in a companion report (Rollison et al., forthcoming). The second study, which is the subject of this report, is a review of secondary data, programs, and policies to understand clinical practices and TRICARE requirements associated with the use of intensive outpatient programs to treat active-duty service members affected by the mental health consequences of sexual harassment and sexual assault that occurred while serving in the military.

This research followed standard human subject protection regulations and DoD regulations governing human subjects research. Interview subjects consented to being identified by name in the report. Their views are their own and do not represent the official policy or position of DoD or the U.S. Government.

RAND National Security Research Division

The research reported here was completed in August 2021 and underwent security review with the sponsor and the Defense Office of Prepublication and Security Review before public release.

This research was sponsored by the Defense Health Agency Psychological Health Center of Excellence and conducted within the Forces and

Resources Policy Center of the RAND National Security Research Division (NSRD), which operates the National Defense Research Institute (NDRI), a federally funded research and development center sponsored by the Office of the Secretary of Defense, the Joint Staff, the Unified Combatant Commands, the Navy, the Marine Corps, the defense agencies, and the defense intelligence enterprise.

For more information on the RAND Forces and Resources Policy Center, see www.rand.org/nsrd/frp or contact the director (contact information is provided on the webpage).

Acknowledgments

The authors would like to thank the sponsor of this work, specifically, PHCoE's Holly O'Reilly for her communications and information that were critical to the success of this effort. We also thank Michaele McKeever-Davis and Michelle Glaser at TRICARE and Kyrstyna Bienia and Ed Simmer at DHA Medical Affairs for their support throughout the research effort. We are grateful to the clinicians and program staff who generously shared their time, experiences, and insights with us. We are grateful for the review and input from Barbara Bicksler and for the quality assurance reviews from Lisa Jaycox, Charles Engel, Molly McIntosh, John Winkler, and Jim Powers that served to improve this report.

Summary

Issue

The fiscal year (FY) 2019 National Defense Authorization Act (NDAA), Section 702, directed the U.S. Department of Defense (DoD) to "carry out a pilot program to assess the feasibility and advisability of using intensive outpatient treatment programs to treat members of the Armed Forces suffering from posttraumatic stress disorder [PTSD] resulting from military sexual trauma, including treatment for substance abuse, depression, and other issues related to such conditions" (Public Law 115-232, 2018). The Psychological Health Center of Excellence (PHCoE) commissioned the RAND Corporation's National Defense Research Institute to conduct supplemental analysis to support its response to Congress.

Topics and Approach

PHCoE asked RAND researchers to examine three research topics:

1. An analysis of data from the military workplace on the prevalence of sexual trauma among personnel with mental health conditions.
2. A programmatic review of four intensive outpatient programs (IOPs)—two in the private sector and two in DoD—to understand different program components available to active-duty service members who have experienced sexual trauma and other trauma.
3. A review of policies to understand TRICARE authorization procedures and other regulations governing IOPs.

To conduct this research, we examined data from the 2014 RAND Military Workplace Study survey, reviewed relevant policies, and interviewed personnel from IOPs to obtain contextual information to inform PHCoE's response to Congress.

Key Findings

- Our secondary data analysis revealed that, in a hypothetical group of 100 servicewomen with probable PTSD, we would expect that 40 had been sexually assaulted in their lifetimes. For 15 of the 40, they would have been sexually assaulted within the previous year.
- The demand for services is a key driver of decisions about how, when, and where to implement an IOP model of care. If a clinic or hospital serves a large enough group of service members with PTSD, it might be able to support specialized sexual trauma–informed care.
- Using our programmatic review, private-sector and direct-care IOP programs use evidence-based treatment approaches and have established processes for treating active-duty service members.
- Our policy review and discussions with program officials indicated that the TRICARE application process, accreditation, state licensing, and credentialing were not identified as barriers to private-sector IOP authorization and practice. Other policies, related to reimbursement, referral, leave, and privacy, were identified as potential barriers.

Knowledge Gaps

Our reviews revealed many knowledge gaps surrounding the experiences, treatment needs, and the effectiveness of different treatment components and models of care for active-duty victims of sexual harassment and sexual assault experiencing PTSD and related mental health problems. These knowledge gaps suggest additional areas of study for PHCoE and DHA to explore to further their understanding of this important topic.

What are the treatment preferences of active-duty victims of sexual harassment and sexual assault with psychological health needs?
Our analysis highlights the need to collect data on the preferences of this population for seeking care in the private sector versus direct care at a military treatment facility (MTF). Furthermore, it would be useful to understand why certain active-duty service members may prefer a private-sector IOP; understanding those reasons may help the DoD improve care at MTFs.

Are IOPs effective? If so, what makes them effective? Are they more effective than traditional outpatient treatment for active-duty service members who have experienced sexual harassment or sexual assault during military service?

More research is needed before implementing the IOP model as a standard of care. It would be important to understand whether the benefits of IOP care relative to traditional outpatient level of care are enough to warrant the increased cost of implementing and relying on IOPs for the targeted patient population. The experts with whom we spoke and the literature we reviewed raise other important hypotheses and areas of study, such as whether attrition rates or key features of an IOP (e.g., group therapy) predict the IOP's effectiveness. An evaluation would identify the key predictors of treatment outcomes, the trade-offs associated with rolling or cohort-based admissions, and where to host an IOP.

Is DoD equipped to meet the psychological health need(s) of these service members?

Determining current utilization rates of outpatient DoD and private-sector IOPs is a starting point. DHA should assess the ability of DoD to meet the demand for IOP care among active-duty service members who have experienced sexual trauma and the availability of private-sector or U.S. Department of Veterans Affairs (VA) IOPs should DoD's capacity fall short.

Further Considerations for the DHA

DHA might consider establishing a research roadmap for how best to address these and other knowledge gaps about the optimal treatment for active-duty service members with problems stemming from a military sexual assault. Some key topics, as summarized in Table S.1, consist of treatment effectiveness, patient preferences, and military health system (MHS) and TRICARE capacity. A necessary next step would be consideration of clinical management and care coordination policies and procedures, particularly when referrals are made to private-sector programs. In our policy review, we did not identify standardized guidance for referring clinicians,

TABLE S.1
Topics for Future Research

Approach	Research Areas
Treatment effectiveness	
Program evaluation	Assess multiple program components, such as program length, treatment approaches, group size, and location Standardize clinical procedures to enhance evaluation
Comparative effectiveness trials	Compare outpatient programs with IOPs Compare direct-care with private-sector or VA outpatient and IOP
Patient preferences	
Interview and survey	Assess preferences for types of therapy, length, and setting Consider preferences in subpopulations (e.g., at-risk groups)
MHS and TRICARE capacity	
Cost benefit analysis	Determine demand for services Assess availability of services in MTFs and the private sector Assess cost implications of treatment delivered in MTFs, VA, and private sector Consider transaction costs of partnering with non-DoD organizations
Clinical management	
Provider assessment	Evaluate clinical coordination procedures (e.g., referral, medical charting, discharge plans)
Care coordination	Assess whether clear policies and procedures exist and are accessible for behavioral health providers to refer, communicate with private-sector program staff, and receive service members back for additional treatment
Policy analysis	Assess appropriateness of existing travel and lodging reimbursement procedures

but additional research to assess the availability of clear policies and procedures for behavioral health providers is needed.

A systematic evaluation of the topics we have described is a necessary next step to understanding the appropriateness of utilizing IOPs to treat service members' mental health consequences of experiencing sexual trauma in the military. The review described in this report highlights the promising outcomes of IOPs and suggests that DoD should continue to evaluate the use of these programs to treat service members experiencing mental health consequences of sexual trauma.

Contents

Figures and Tables

Figures

Tables

CHAPTER ONE

Introduction

The fiscal year (FY) 2019 National Defense Authorization Act (NDAA), Section 702, directed the U.S. Department of Defense (DoD) to "carry out a pilot program to assess the feasibility and advisability of using intensive outpatient treatment programs to treat members of the Armed Forces suffering from posttraumatic stress disorder resulting from military sexual trauma, including treatment for substance abuse, depression, and other issues related to such conditions." That pilot study "shall be carried out through partnerships with public, private, and non-profit health care organizations, universities, and institutions that meet specific criteria" (Public Law 115-232, 2018).

The pilot conducted by DoD was open to TRICARE-authorized intensive outpatient programs (IOPs) that use only "evidence-based treatment strategies for the treatment of diagnoses associated with a disclosed sexual trauma. Treatment may include . . . individual and/or group psychotherapy and psychoeducation" (TRICARE Policy Manual 6010.59-M, Chapter 18, Section 8, 2020). The pilot was scheduled to end August 31, 2021, with patients being enrolled as late as July 31, 2021 (TRICARE, 2021b).

In response to this authorization, the Defense Health Agency (DHA) Psychological Health Center of Excellence (PHCoE) and TRICARE are conducting a two-part study to describe current DoD practices for posttraumatic stress disorder (PTSD) treatment (outpatient programs and IOPs) and to assess treatment effectiveness among five participating private-sector IOPs and two DoD IOPs. Ultimately, two private-sector IOPs from the East Region, under the same corporate umbrella, three private-sector IOPs from the West Region, and two Army Medical Centers took part in the pilot (TRICARE, 2021b).

To assist with its response to Congress, PHCoE commissioned the RAND Corporation's National Defense Research Institute to conduct supplemental analysis of secondary data, programs, and policies.[1] More specifically, PHCoE asked RAND researchers to address three disparate topics:

1. **An analysis of the prevalence of sexual trauma among service members experiencing PTSD or depression.** From the 2014 RAND Military Workplace Survey, we estimated the proportion of service members with probable PTSD or depression who have experienced sexual harassment or sexual assault in the past year. These estimates serve as a basis for determining the need for sexual trauma–informed care for service members.

2. **A programmatic review of select IOPs** (two private-sector programs and two operated by DoD) to understand different program components available to active-duty service members who have experienced sexual trauma and other trauma.[2] We held discussions with staff at medical centers, hospitals, and clinics to talk about program processes and components and solicit their views on barriers and facilitators to active-duty service members receiving effective treatment. However, these reviews were not an evaluation of the programs themselves.

3. **A review of policies to understand barriers to service members participating in IOPs.** We analyzed publicly available policies, such as TRICARE and other related policies, as they relate to active-duty service members referred to IOPs, both at DoD military treatment facilities (MTFs), known as *direct care*, and at civilian facilities through the TRICARE network, known as *private-sector care*.[3] We

---

[1] RAND researchers also conducted three evidence synthesis reviews focused on the barriers and facilitators to treatment and the treatment effectiveness for mental health consequences for service members who disclose sexual assault. The findings from that effort are described in a companion to this report (Rollison et al., forthcoming).

[2] In identifying IOPs for its review, we excluded those IOPs participating in DoD's pilot study. Appendix B contains details of the selection approach.

[3] Private-sector care used to be known as *purchased care*.

supplemented the policy review with information gleaned during discussions with IOP clinicians and administrators.

A more detailed discussion of the approach used to address each of these topics is described in the respective chapters and associated appendixes. Before reporting on the results of our research, we provide definitions of relevant terminology and brief overviews of sexual trauma and mental health, PTSD treatment approaches, models of mental health care delivery, and the treatment of PTSD in the military to orient the reader to the following chapters.

Terminology

The legal, scientific, and clinical terminology used to define sexual harassment and sexual assault require attention and precision. Legal statutes define what constitutes sexual assault, and these definitions vary by state. The Uniform Code of Military Justice (UCMJ) defines criminal offenses under military law and is therefore the primary source of our terminology (10 U.S.C. Sections 801–940, 1958).

DoD Directive 6495.01, 2012, provides a definition of sexual assault that is consistent with 10 U.S.C. Section 920, Article 120. When we use the term *sexual assault*, we mean,

> Intentional sexual contact characterized by use of force, threats, intimidation, or abuse of authority or when the victim does not or cannot consent. Sexual assault defined by the military includes a broad category of sexual offenses consisting of the following specific UCMJ offenses: rape, sexual assault, aggravated sexual contact, abusive sexual contact, forcible sodomy (forced oral or anal sex), or attempts to commit these acts (DoD Directive 6495.01, 2012).

Sexual harassment in the military context is defined in 10 U.S.C. Section 934, Article 134 and in DoD Directive 1350.2 as

> a form of sex discrimination that involves unwelcome sexual advances, requests for sexual favors, and other verbal or physical conduct of a sexual nature when:

- submission to such conduct is made either explicitly or implicitly a term or condition of a person's job, pay, or career, or submission to or rejection of such conduct by a person is used as a basis for career or employment decisions affecting that person, or
- Such conduct has the purpose or effect of unreasonably interfering with an individual's work performance or creates an intimidating, hostile, or offensive working environment). Sexual harassment includes a sexually hostile work environment, sexual quid pro quo, and gender discrimination (DoD Directive 1350.2, 2015).[4]

The term *military sexual trauma* is used by the Veterans Health Administration (VHA) to refer to severe or threatening forms of sexual harassment or sexual assault that occurred during military service. The term is defined as a "physical assault of a sexual nature, battery of a sexual nature, or sexual harassment ["repeated, unsolicited verbal or physical contact of a sexual nature which is threatening in character"] that occurred while a Veteran was serving on active duty or active duty for training" (38 U.S.C., § 1720D). The U.S. Department of Veterans Affairs (VA) conducts mandatory military sexual trauma screening that captures experiences of severe sexual harassment and sexual assault. In this report, we reserve the term military sexual trauma for VA assessment procedures and related research.

Trauma and Mental Health

More than 40 years of research has consistently associated adult sexual harassment and sexual assault with increased risk of broad deleterious mental health symptoms and conditions (Dworkin et al., 2017) among both civilian (Chivers-Wilson, 2006; Kilpatrick and Acierno, 2003; Kilpatrick et al., 2007) and military populations. Yet, as with all trauma exposure, (Kimerling et al., 2007; Newins et al., 2020) not all individuals who experi-

---

[4] The military definition of *sexual harassment* was updated between the start and completion of this study. The December 29, 2020, update of DoDI 1020.03 contains the most recent definition. We have retained the earlier definition in the table for consistency with the guidance available at study inception.

ence sexual harassment or sexual assault develop PTSD (Atwoli, 2015). Estimates suggest that 17 percent to 65 percent of civilian adult sexual assault survivors develop PTSD at some point in their lifetimes (Campbell et al., 2009, and Kessler et al., 1999).

People with PTSD often also meet the criteria for depression and substance use disorders (Grant et al., 2016, and Xu et al., 2013), with comorbid prevalence rates of 35 percent and 46 percent, respectively (Pietrzak et al., 2011). The relationship between PTSD and depression or substance use disorders is complex and often bidirectional (Campbell et al., 2009, and Gong et al., 2019), which can make these comorbidities challenging to treat. Patients with concurrent PTSD and either depression or substance use disorders show higher symptom severity, greater functional impairment, and poorer treatment outcomes compared with patients with either disorder alone (Knowles et al., 2019; McCauley et al., 2012; Spinhoven et al., 2014).

PTSD Treatments

Clinical practice guidelines prescribe evidence-based practices to treat specific conditions. The VA/DoD clinical practice guidelines for PTSD strongly recommend individual, manualized, trauma-focused psychotherapy as the primary treatment approach for people with PTSD. This approach includes specific cognitive behavioral therapy (CBT), prolonged exposure (PE) therapy, eye movement desensitization and reprocessing (EMDR), brief eclectic psychotherapy, narrative exposure therapy, and written narrative exposure (VA and DoD, 2017).[5] Pharmacotherapy (e.g., selective serotonin reuptake inhibitors or serotonin-norepinephrine reuptake inhibitors) is recommended when individual trauma-focused psychotherapy is not readily available or when patients elect not to engage in such treatment (VA and DoD, 2017). The American Psychological Association's recommended evidence-based psychotherapies and pharmacotherapy options for PTSD (Craske, 2017) overlap significantly with the VA/DoD's clinical practice guidelines. Neither provides treatment recommendations based on the different types of trauma that may lead to PTSD (e.g., natural disaster, sudden loss of a

---

[5] See Appendix C for summaries of these and other common treatment approaches.

loved one, sexual assault, or combat), although clinical research is typically conducted with either victims of sexual trauma or combat veterans.

Models of Mental Health Care Delivery

Mental health care can be described as occurring or being delivered on a continuum, which includes IOP and ranges from primary care to inpatient hospitalization (see Figure 1.1). Many individuals with PTSD and other behavioral health disorders first present in primary care rather than specialty mental health care settings (Schnurr et al., 2013). The collaborative care model, often referred to as *integrated care*, was developed as a method to address mental health in primary care settings rather than immediately referring patients out to specialty care. The approach integrates physical and mental health services that together work to manage mental health disorders as a chronic disease rather than treating acute symptoms (Thielke, Vannoy, and Unützer, 2007; Unützer et al., 2006, and Unützer et al., 2013). This model typically uses a stepped-care approach to manage mental health conditions such that the most effective, yet least resource-intensive treatment, is delivered first.

Depending on the level of patient distress, need, and success with initial low-intensity intervention, a patient may subsequently be stepped up to more intensive and complex treatment involving additional care delivery modalities (e.g., group therapy) and appropriate specialists (e.g., psychia-

FIGURE 1.1
Continuum of Mental Health Care

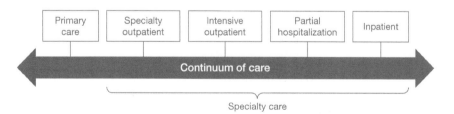

6

trists). Care coordination between the referring primary care provider and newly integrated mental health specialists is essential to the collaborative care model, which has been shown to improve PTSD and depression symptoms among combat-exposed service members (Engel et al., 2016).

In addition, there is some evidence that collaborative care can increase patient adherence to treatment, improve patient satisfaction, and potentially reduce premature termination from treatment (Craske et al., 2011; Fortney et al., 2015; Meredith et al., 2016; Peek, 2013; Schnurr et al., 2013; Zatzick et al., 2013, and Zatzick et al., 2015).

The VA/DoD clinical practice guidelines for the treatment of PTSD in primary care indicate collaborative care interventions has weak evidence as an evidence-based approach to improving patient engagement with mental health care (VA and DoD, 2017). And the CPG underscores the fact that comorbid conditions should be considered when determining a treatment plan.

Primary and Specialty Outpatient Care

When the first-line mental health care delivered in primary care settings is not successful in providing symptom reduction or remission, VA/DoD clinical practice guidelines for PTSD management recommends that patients receive specialty outpatient treatment or therapy. These 45- to 90-minute sessions are typically delivered by a licensed social worker or clinical psychologist on a weekly basis and should align with an evidence-based treatment, such as CBT or PE (VA and DoD, 2017). However, even when these guidelines for specialty outpatient treatment are followed, success is not guaranteed.

For example, anywhere from 30 percent to 62 percent of patients receiving exposure-based therapies drop out of care before they can experience significant symptom reduction (Kehle-Forbes et al., 2016, and Mott et al., 2014). A variety of reasons account for the high rate of attrition in outpatient settings. One of the primary reasons is emblematic of the PTSD condition itself—avoidance. The avoidance cluster of PTSD symptoms is characterized by attempts to avoid distressing emotions, thoughts, and memories and also activities, people, or physical places that serve as reminders of the traumatic event. Promising new treatments are emerging, such as written exposure therapy (WET), that are briefer (five sessions for WET), easier to deliver, and result in much lower dropout rate (6 percent for WET) (Thompson-Hollands et al., 2019).

Intensive Outpatient Programming

The next level of care, intensive outpatient programming, is defined by TRI-CARE as "an outpatient level of care that provides an organized day or evening program for the treatment of mental health and/or substance use disorders (SUDs) . . . care typically consists of between six and nine or more hours a week of treatment services (minimum two hours per treatment day) which includes assessment, treatment, and rehabilitation" (TRICARE Policy Manual 6010.60-M, Chapter 7, Section 3.16, 2018). IOPs provide the opportunity for a therapeutic dose of treatment within a condensed time frame. It may be more appealing for a patient to buy into the idea of approaching rather than avoiding distressing thoughts, memories, and emotions for a few weeks versus a few months, especially if symptom improvement follows the same time frame trajectory (Sherrill et al., 2020).

Quicker paths to recovery have been noted as especially important factors for military populations who may be reticent to commit to longer-term treatments because of employment and family responsibilities or deployment and duty-station changes (Yasinski et al., 2018). In this way, targeting PTSD within an IOP framework does not necessarily require a stepping up of care because of symptom severity or lack of success with lower-intensity care delivery modalities—but this method may be initiated based on patient preferences and provider judgment to increase access to care, reduce barriers associated with avoidance and attrition, and improve outcomes in PTSD treatment (Ragsdale et al., 2020).

Research and clinical practice efforts have begun condensing exposure-based therapies or cognitive processing therapy (CPT) for PTSD into an IOP format of two- to three-week treatment duration, often with additional or adjunctive services such as group therapy, art therapy, family services, yoga, or other wellness interventions (Beidel, Frueh et al., 2017; Harvey et al., 2017; Hendriks et al., 2018; Rauch et al., 2021; Yasinski et al., 2018, and Zalta et al., 2018). A review of 11 exposure-based treatment studies and two CPT-focused studies within an IOP format revealed similar positive outcomes as specialty outpatient treatment but with dramatically increased completion rates (often approximating greater than 95 percent) (Ragsdale et al., 2020). That is, the therapy works just as well, but in this format, many more people are able to complete the program and benefit from it.

As an illustrative example, the Wounded Warrior Project funds four academic medical centers known as the Warrior Care Network. Each center developed two- to three-week IOPs that treat PTSD among post-9/11 veterans and service members (Harvey et al., 2017). Each program includes slightly different components, such as integrative therapies and wellness programming to support maintenance of gains and increased general functioning, but are consistent in their use of IOP case management, peer support, and evidence-based anchor treatments for PTSD, including CPT and PE.

The average treatment completion rate reported by Harvey and colleagues was 95 percent across the four sites, and patients reported high satisfaction (greater than 90 percent) as measured by agreement with several statements (e.g., "Overall, I feel satisfied with the clinical care I have received" and "The care I received has improved the problem(s) I needed help with.") Where available, site-specific outcome research included the following:

- 77 percent of IOP completers across 13 studies of both veteran and nonveteran samples experienced clinically significant PTSD symptom reduction, with 44 percent losing their probable PTSD diagnosis (Rauch et al., 2020)
- 88 percent of 270 IOP completers maintained treatment gains at a 12-month follow-up (Burton et al., 2019)
- The Warrior Care Network reported on 325 patients and found significant reduction in PTSD and depression symptoms upon program completion (Harvey et al., 2019).

This evidence from efficacy and effectiveness trials of IOPs for PTSD, which are frequently composed of U.S. military personnel and veterans, is encouraging. Results indicate high retention rates, positive clinical outcomes, and high patient satisfaction. Yet, this is not to say there are no drawbacks to this care modality. A qualitative study of 25 veteran patient perceptions regarding the intensive structure of treatment found the majority of patient reactions were positive, some also acknowledged that the intensity caused short-term discomfort (i.e., emotional distress, exhaustion, and frustration) and was demanding in terms of effort and time (Sherrill et al., 2020). Further research is needed to better understand patient-level characteristics and preferences related to IOPs for PTSD, including research about patients who drop out of treatment or do not benefit from the intensive structure.

Partial-Hospitalization Programs and Inpatient Care

Next along the continuum is partial-hospitalization programs (PHPs), which are a middle ground between IOP and inpatient care.[6] PHPs are day programs designed for patients with significant or still severe behavioral health symptoms who need a structured treatment program but do not need 24-hour supervision. A PHP is typically four to six hours per day and as frequent as five days per week.

Inpatient hospitalization, the most intensive level of care, is a structured setting with 24-hour care, usually for patients whose mental health symptoms (1) now include actively suicidal or homicidal thoughts or actions, or (2) pose a threat to their own safety (e.g., by being unable to maintain adequate nutrition or hygiene) or the safety of others. Patients are usually stepped down from this level of care when they no longer pose a threat to themselves or to others. That is, full resolution of all symptoms is not necessary for discharge.

Treatment Retention Among Service Members with PTSD

Even when evidence-based treatments for PTSD are available, they can only be helpful if service members are able to remain engaged in treatment. Mental health systems (MHSs) must be able to not only provide patients with

---

[6] These programs are categorized as a time-limited, ambulatory, active treatment that offers therapeutically intensive, coordinated, and structured clinical services within a stable therapeutic environment. Partial hospitalization is an appropriate setting for crisis stabilization, treatment of partially stabilized mental health disorders, including substance disorders, and a transition from an inpatient program when medically necessary (TRICARE Policy Manual 6010.60-M, Chapter 11, Section 2.5, 2017).

initial care but must also retain those patients for long enough to achieve significant symptom reduction or remission. According to a retrospective study of active-duty service members who received PTSD care at military outpatient clinics, we can expect that the largest reduction in PTSD symptom severity will occur during the first eight treatment encounters (Hoyt and Edwards-Stewart, 2018). However, retention for this length of time is not the norm. Among service members who are diagnosed with PTSD in the MHS, nearly one-quarter (24 percent) do not receive any psychotherapy *or* pharmacotherapy recommended by clinical practice guidelines during the four months following their diagnosis (Hepner et al., 2021). For those patients who do receive PTSD care within a year of their diagnosis, 35 percent did not receive the number of psychotherapy sessions recommended to achieve symptom reduction (Hepner et al., 2017).

It may be that the type of psychotherapy offered contributes to whether patients decide to remain engaged in care. For example, trauma-focused treatments often include the difficult work of exposure and habituation to trauma memories, which help extinguish fear responses. The treatments are effective but also emotionally challenging for PTSD patients. A systematic review examined PTSD treatment dropout rates in randomized controlled trials of active-duty service members and veterans and revealed that trauma-focused treatments have a dropout rate of 27.1 percent compared with a 16.1 percent dropout rate for nontrauma focused treatments (Hoyt and Edwards-Stewart, 2018). The authors suggested that treatment type rather than population or other variables might be what affects dropout. Dropout may also be due, in part, to *spontaneous remission*. Some service members may recover from PTSD without formal intervention.

Although our understanding of the drivers of treatment retention remains incomplete, the existing findings also point to opportunities for improvement in policy strategies that could increase access to, utilization of, and quality of treatment for service members with PTSD (Committee on the Assessment of Ongoing Efforts in the Treatment of Posttraumatic Stress Disorder, 2014). For example, military training and occupational requirements might make it challenging for service members to regularly seek care during the duty day (even for just an hour or two) on a weekly basis as required for typical, specialty outpatient care. In Hoyt and Edwards-Stewart, 2018, the authors explained that in the military context, "the completion of a course of treatment in a limited number of encounters could have a significant impact on military readiness, allowing patients to return to full duty." The IOP model of delivering care within a prespecified time frame is consistent with the authors' conclusions that concentrated treatment for PTSD, potentially scheduled between required field training or combat deployments, could support service members' return to duty (Hoyt and Edwards-Stewart, 2018).

A companion report on the effectiveness of treatments for victims of sexual trauma found that skills-based treatments were equally or more effective than trauma-focused treatments (Rollison et al., forthcoming). The effectiveness of different psychotherapeutic approaches to treating PTSD remains an active area of study, and one that is important for designing treatment programs that minimize treatment dropout.

Organization of This Report

The next three chapters address each of the topics that we were asked to examine. In Chapter Two, we describe data analysis conducted to understand sexual trauma history in service members with probable PTSD or probable depression. In Chapter Three, we summarize our discussions with DoD and private-sector IOP personnel and what we learned from the program materials we reviewed. In Chapter Four, we present TRICARE policies for IOPs and discuss program administrators' experiences implementing those policies. The report ends with observations of knowledge gaps in the use of IOPs to treat service members who experienced sexual harassment or sexual assault in the military, and we identify additional research that is needed to inform the feasibility and the advisability of this treatment approach.

CHAPTER TWO

Sexual Harassment, Sexual Assault, and Mental Health in the Military

As described in Chapter One, PHCoE's first topic of interest was to assess the prevalence of sexual trauma among service members with mental health conditions. In this chapter, we report estimates of the proportion of service members with probable PTSD and depression who have experienced sexual trauma. Before turning to these estimates, we begin with a discussion of sexual harassment and sexual assault in the military—what they mean and how they differ from sexual harassment and sexual assault in the general population.

Characterizing Sexual Harassment and Sexual Assault That Occurred During Military Service

Sexual harassment in the military context has a precise policy definition that includes, among other requirements, unwelcome sexual advances, requests, and offensive comments or gestures with a nexus to the target's job, pay, or career that are so severe or pervasive that a reasonable person, including the victim, would perceive the work environment as hostile or offensive (10 U.S.C. Section 934, Article 134, 2016; DoD Directive 1350.2, 2015).

This definition differs from some lay interpretations of the term *sexual harassment* in that it does not include events that occur outside the workplace (e.g., sexual heckling on a public street), consensual interactions between coworkers in which neither party is offended (e.g., two employees sharing a sexual joke out of earshot of other coworkers), or normative social encounters (e.g., two colleague hugging after not seeing each other for a week). Rather, the requirements make clear that the behavior is unwanted, offensive, and creates a hostile work environment for the target.

The UCMJ Section 120 provides a detailed description of the legal definition of sexual assault that includes specific physical acts, the intent of the perpetrator, and the form of coercion that together are used to categorize an event as unlawful. The military context of sexual assault often differs in important ways from sexual assaults that occur among the general population. For civilians, sexual assault typically occurs in the context of romantic or sexual relationships and occurs in residential settings, often in the victim's or the perpetrator's home (Reddington and Wright Kreisel, 2017). Alcohol use—by the victim, perpetrator, or both—is common (Lorenz and Ullman, 2016), and women are far more likely than men to be victimized, particularly in adulthood (Reddington and Wright Kreisel, 2017). To the extent that there is a "typical" assault among civilians, it would be perpetrated by a man against a woman with whom he was romantically involved, in a private setting, involving alcohol use, and with minimal force.

In contrast, assaults against military service members often occur at work during duty hours, while percentages of sexual assault at work with no alcohol involved are much higher for men than for women; about one third of victims report they had been drinking at the time of the assault and that about 37 percent of offenders had been drinking at the time of the assault (Morral, Gore, and Schell, 2015).

Commonly, the perpetrator(s) is also a service member who work in the same occupation or location, and only rarely is the offender an intimate partner (Jaycox et al., 2014). Although servicewomen are 8.9 times more likely to be sexually assaulted than servicemen, there is still a large number of male victims annually (approximately 7,500; Breslin et al., 2019). Compared with assaults against servicewomen, assaults against servicemen more often result in physical injuries. They are often perpetrated by multiple offenders (usually men), repeated more than once, and are more likely to be committed with the intention of abusing, humiliating, or hazing the victim (Jaycox et al., 2014; Morral, Gore, and Schell, 2015). Service members who identify as lesbian, gay, or bisexual or who do not identify as straight are particularly likely to be targeted; they account for only 12 percent of all service members, but 43 percent of all sexual assault victims (Morral and Schell, 2021).

It is important to understand the differences between *typical* civilian sexual assaults and sexual assaults that occur in the military prior to providing mental health services to service members who have survived a sexual assault. Mental health providers with expertise in treating sexual assault in civilian settings may have developed their approach and clinical skill to support victims recovering from an assault perpetrated by a date or significant other. Clinical tasks may involve rejecting cognitive distortions in which the victim believes themselves to be responsible because they were drinking. Victims may need help recovering an ability to trust an intimate partner.

Certainly, for some sexual assault victims in the military, the context of their assault will match this prototype and a similar clinical approach may be necessary. However, for many others, that may not be appropriate. Mental health providers should be prepared to treat victims for whom the sexual assault was an extreme form of workplace sexual harassment—perpetrated by multiple, often male, colleagues during the workday and in the victim's duty station. They may have been targeted because they are—or because the perpetrator(s) perceived them to be—gay, lesbian, or bisexual. Clinical tasks may include recovery from the betrayal of being victimized by a fellow service member, the stigma and shame of being a victim when a service member's identity and training prioritizes strength, and possible related damage to the victim's military career (Morral et al., 2021).

Estimating Prevalence of PTSD, Depression, Sexual Harassment, and Sexual Assault

Although there is a broad literature that estimates the proportion of sexual assault victims who go on to develop mental health conditions like PTSD or depression (Dworkin et al., 2017), it has been rare to approach the association from the opposite direction. That is, among individuals with mental health conditions, what proportion have experienced sexual harassment or sexual assault?

The answer to this question would be useful to mental health administrators and providers who may need to estimate the proportion of their patient population who might benefit from sexual trauma informed care. If the estimate is very low, it may not be feasible or cost effective to establish specialized tracks or programs for victims of sexual trauma. A single clinical expert could cover the need. However, if the estimate is substantial, some systems or organizations should consider providing specialized programs.

To better understand whether the MHS should prioritize specialized services for victims of sexual harassment or sexual assault, we completed a secondary analysis of data from the 2014 RAND Military Workplace Survey (Morral, Gore, and Schell, 2015).

This survey provides population level estimates of PTSD and depression combined with assessments of sexual harassment and sexual assault in the military. We used these data to estimate the proportion of service members with probable PTSD or depression who had also experienced sexual harassment or sexual assault and, thus, might benefit from access to mental health services that are specialized for sexual trauma recovery.

The sample frame for the survey was all active-duty service members excluding those with fewer than six months of service, general and flag officers, and those under age 18. All active-duty women and 25 percent of active-duty servicemen were invited to participate, and 30.4 percent of the sample did so. Survey weights were used to account for the sampling design and survey nonresponse using 40 administrative variables that assessed sociodemographic, occupational, and survey fieldwork information. A complete description of the study design and implementation is available elsewhere (Morral, Gore, and Schell, 2014; Morral, Gore, and Schell, 2015).

RAND Military Workplace Survey Measures

The 2014 RAND Military Workplace Survey measure of *sexual assault* was designed to align closely with legal criteria in the UCMJ Article 120 (Rape and Sexual Assault). A nested, three-part series of questions assess whether an event in the past year satisfied all UCMJ criteria for sexual assaults: (1) an unwanted experience occurred like one described in the law (e.g., unwanted penetration of an orifice), (2) the event was intended to abuse or humiliate the victim or done to gratify a sexual desire, and (3) one of the UCMJ-defined coercive actions was used (e.g., threats, force, alcohol incapacitation) (Jaycox et al., 2014).

The 2014 RAND Military Workplace Survey measure of *sexual harassment* was designed to align closely with the DoD definition of *sexual harass-*

ment included in DoD Directive 1350.2. The measure begins with behaviorally specific screening items, which, when endorsed, are followed by questions ascertaining whether (1) any such experience continued despite the coworker knowing that the respondent was upset by it or (2) it was sufficiently offensive that most members of the military would be offended by it. Individuals who indicated that their experience met these criteria were classified as having experienced sexual harassment in the past year (Jaycox et al., 2014).

PTSD was assessed using the Primary Care PTSD Screen for DSM-5 (PC-PTSD), a five-item measure using the criteria from the *Diagnostic and Statistical Manual of Mental Disorders* (DSM). The scale has strong diagnostic accuracy (Area Under the Curve = 0.94) as tested with a veteran sample (Prins et al., 2016). Scale scores range from 0 to 5, and in accordance with recommendations, we used a cut score of 3 to optimize scale sensitivity (Prins et al., 2016). Without confirmation by a diagnostic interview to establish a diagnosis of PTSD, we cannot be certain that all service members who scored above the scale threshold met all criteria for PTSD. Thus, throughout this report, we describe the group of service members who screened positive via their PC-PTSD score as experiencing probable PTSD.

Depression was assessed using the Patient Health Questionnaire (PHQ-8) (Kroenke et al., 2009). The scale has good sensitivity and specificity when used to identify depression (Kroenke et al., 2010). The eight-item scale ranges from 0 to 24, and in accordance with the recommendation, we used a cut score of 10 to identify a moderate depression symptoms and 15 to identify severe depressive symptoms. Without confirmation by a diagnostic interview to establish a diagnosis of major depressive disorder, we cannot be certain that all service members who scored above the scale threshold met all criteria for diagnosis.

Thus, as for PTSD, we describe the group of service members who screened positive for depression via PHQ score, as experiencing *probable moderate depression or probable severe depression.*

In combination, we produced descriptive statistics to estimate the following:

1. The proportion of service members categorized as experiencing probable PTSD who had been
    a. sexually harassed in the past year

    b.   sexually assaulted in the past year, in their military career, or prior to their military service.

2.   The proportion of service members categorized as experiencing probable depression who had been

    a.   sexually harassed in the past year

    b.   sexually assaulted in the past year, in their military career, or prior to their military service.

In accordance with standards set in our initial evaluation of 2014 RAND Military Workplace Survey data (Morral, Gore, and Schell, 2015), cell values within tables were specified as "not reportable" (NR) when they were calculated within groups smaller than 15 respondents or when the margin of error was greater than 15 percentage points. We initially planned to examine the relationship between PTSD or depression symptoms and the characteristics of the sexual harassment or sexual assault (e.g., recency of the trauma, assault characteristics, offender characteristics, reporting, satisfaction with received services). On review, the tables describing subanalyses for sexual assault all included NR data. Some tables describing subanalyses for sexual harassment were reportable for women only, but without the comparison across gender and trauma type, they offer limited clinical utility. Thus, these subanalyses are not included in the report.

Sexual Harassment and Sexual Assault Among Military Services Members with Probable PTSD

Compared with servicewomen who were not categorized as experiencing probable PTSD, servicewomen with probable PTSD were 2.3 times more likely to also be categorized as having been sexually harassed within the prior year (Table 2.1). The finding for servicemen was similar: those with symptoms suggestive of probable PTSD were 2.6 times more likely to be categorized as having been sexually harassed in the past year compared with men without PTSD. Overall, 39.9 percent of women and 14.7 percent of men with symptoms suggestive of probable PTSD had experiences consistent with sexual harassment within the prior year.

Among service members categorized as experiencing probable PTSD, 15.1 percent of women and 1.9 percent of men were also categorized as having been *sexually assaulted* in the past year (Table 2.1). Among women, those with symptoms suggestive of probable PTSD were 5.6 times more likely than servicewomen without this level of symptoms to be categorized as having experienced a sexual assault in the past year. For men, the percentage who experienced a sexual assault in the past year did not differ significantly between those with and without symptoms suggestive of probable PTSD. Overall, 39.5 percent of servicewomen and 5.8 percent of servicemen with symptoms suggestive of probable PTSD had been sexually assaulted at some point in their lifetimes.

TABLE 2.1

Percentage of Service Members Who Were Categorized as Having Experienced a Sexual Trauma, by Gender and Probable PTSD

Sexual Trauma		Women		Men	
		Without PTSD (%)	Probable PTSD (%)	Without PTSD (%)	Probable PTSD(%)
Sexual harassment	Within the prior year	17.4 (16.2–18.6)	39.9 (36.4–43.5)	5.6 (4.5–6.6)	14.7 (11.2–18.2)
	Not in the prior year	82.6 (81.4–83.8)	60.1 (56.5–63.6)	94.4 (93.4–95.5)	85.3 (81.8–88.8)
Sexual assault	Within the prior year	2.7 (2.1–3.2)	15.1 (12–18.1)	0.7 (0.3–1.1)	1.9 (0.5–3.3)
	During military career, but not in the prior year	7.4 (6.7–8.1)	20.5 (17.9–23.1)	1.0 (0.7–1.3)	2.7 (1.3–4.0)
	Prior to military career only	3.0 (2.5–3.5)	4.0 (2.6–5.4)	0.3 (0.2–0.4)	1.3 (0.1–2.4)
	None	87.0 (86.0–87.9)	60.5 (57.0–64.0)	98.0 (97.5–98.6)	94.2 (92–96.3)

SOURCE: Morral, Gore, and Schell, 2015.
NOTE: 95-percent confidence intervals for each estimate are in parentheses

Sexual Harassment and Sexual Assault Among Military Services Members with Probable Depression

Compared with servicewomen who were not categorized as experiencing probable depression, servicewomen with moderate depression symptoms were 2.0 times more likely and those experiencing severe depression symptoms were 2.4 times more likely to indicate experiences consistent with *sexual harassment* within the prior year (Table 2.2). The odds ratio for men was even higher. Men with moderate or severe depression symptoms were 4.5 to 4.7 times more likely to indicate experience consistent with sexual harassment in the past year compared with men without clinically significant depression symptoms. Overall, 42.8 percent of servicewomen and 21.2 percent of servicemen with severe depression symptoms had experiences consistent with sexual harassment within the prior year.

Among service members with symptoms suggestive of severe depression, 15.9 percent of women and 1.3 percent of men had experienced a *sexual assault* in the past year (Table 2.2). Among women, those with probable severe depression symptoms were 4.8 times more likely than servicewomen not categorized as experiencing depression to have experienced sexual assault in the past year. For men, the percentage who were categorized as having experienced a sexual assault in the past year did not differ significantly between those without depression symptoms relative to those with moderate or severe depression symptoms. Overall, 37.1 percent of servicewomen and 5.4 percent of servicemen with severe depression symptoms had been sexually assaulted at some point in their lifetimes.

Conclusions

According to these descriptive analyses, it appears that many service members who are experiencing clinically significant mental health symptoms suggestive of PTSD and depression have also experienced sexual trauma. For example, in a hypothetical group of 100 female service member with probable PTSD, using the results of our analysis, we would expect that 40 of the 100 women would have been sexually harassed in the prior year and 40 had been sexually assaulted in their lifetimes. Four of these women would have a sexual assault history that occurred prior to joining the military (but

TABLE 2.2
Percentage of Service Members Who Were Categorized as Having Experienced a Sexual Trauma, By Gender and Probable Depression Severity

Sexual Trauma	No Depression (%)	Probable Moderate Depression (%)	Probable Severe Depression (%)	No Depression (%)	Probable Moderate Depression (%)	Probable Severe Depression (%)
Sexual harassment						
Within the prior year	18.1 (16.9–19.3)	35.8 (31.2–40.4)	42.8 (36.7–48.8)	4.5 (3.6–5.3)	20.4 (13.1–27.6)	21.2 (14.2–28.3)
Not in the prior year	81.9 (80.7–83.1)	64.2 (59.6–68.8)	57.2 (51.2–63.3)	95.5 (94.7–96.4)	79.6 (72.4–86.9)	78.8 (71.7–85.8)
Sexual Assault						
Within the prior year	3.3 (2.6–3.9)	10.6 (7.2–13.9)	15.9 (10.5–21.3)	0.6 (0.2–0.9)	3.1 (0–7.2)	1.3 (0.2–2.3)
During military career, but not in the prior year	8.4 (7.7–9.2)	15.4 (12.4–18.3)	18.0 (14.0–22.0)	1.0 (0.7–1.2)	1.8 (0.1–3.5)	3.4 (0.6–6.2)
Prior to military career only	2.9 (2.4–3.3)	6.0 (3.2–8.8)	3.2 (1.4–5.1)	0.3 (0.2–0.5)	0.9 (0.1–1.6)	0.7 (0–1.3)
None	85.4 (84.4–86.4)	68.1 (63.6–72.6)	62.9 (57.0–68.8)	98.1 (97.7–98.6)	94.2 (89.8–98.6)	94.6 (91.6–97.7)

SOURCE: Morral, Gore, and Schell, 2015. NOTE: 95-percent confidence intervals for each estimate are in parentheses.

not after), 21 would have been sexually assaulted during their military service but at least one year prior, and 15 would have been sexually assaulted
within the prior year. Depending on the number of women with PTSD that
a clinic or hospital serves, this could be a large enough group to receive for
specialized, sexual trauma informed care.

Although servicemen are less likely to have experienced a sexual trauma,
the number of servicemen with probable PTSD who have been sexually
harassed or sexually assaulted is non-negligible. In a hypothetical group
of 100 servicemen with probable PTSD using our data analysis, we would
expect that about 15 of the 100 had been sexually harassed in the prior year
and six of them had been sexually assaulted at some point in their lifetimes. Perhaps unsurprising given strong comorbidity between depression
and PTSD (Spinhoven et al., 2014; Stander, Thomsen, and Highfill-McRoy,
2014), we found 5.4 percent of servicemen with severe depression symptoms
had been sexually assaulted at some point in their lifetimes.

An important assumption in these estimates is that sexual trauma victims access care for PTSD or depression at the same rate as others. We
cannot speak directly to whether that assumption is accurate, but previous
analyses of the 2014 RAND Military Workplace Survey data provide some
indication that victims do not always access the response services available
to them (Jaycox et al., 2014). For example, only 15 percent of service members who were sexually assaulted in the past year indicated that they had
talked with a sexual assault response coordinator and only 13 percent had
talked with a victim advocate. Only 13 percent reported seeking services
from a counselor, therapist, or psychologist, and 11 percent sought care
from a medical professional (Jaycox et al., 2014). Across all types of services
that may be used by sexual assault victims, satisfaction with those services
were typically in the moderate range, with the average respondent indicat-
ing that they were "neither satisfied nor dissatisfied" or "satisfied" with the
services they received (Jaycox et al., 2014).

It is possible that more sexual assault victims will seek care in the future,
after more time has elapsed following the trauma. However, it is also important to consider the barriers that may successfully block access to care for
some sexual trauma victims. In an unpublished 2020 review, Julia Rollison
and colleagues completed a scoping review of the literature assessing barriers to care for service members who have experienced sexual harassment or

sexual assault. (Rollison et al., forthcoming). Commonly identified barriers included distrust of the health system, particularly with respect to the confidentiality of records; concern from service members that they will not be believed by providers or support persons; and feelings of stigma or shame.

Ultimately, the decision as to whether the prevalence of sexual harassment and sexual assault in a mental health population is large enough to support the costs and resources to establish a specialized sexual trauma–informed track or program will depend, in large part, on the size of the population and the resources of the organization. We hope that these prevalence estimates can contribute to determining the number of military patients who might benefit from specialized care. If that number is very small, the organization may be better served by referring those patients to external providers. However, as that numbers grows, organizations should consider hiring a provider expert in delivering trauma-informed care or establishing a specialized care program.

CHAPTER THREE

A Review of DoD and Private-Sector Programs

In the second area of inquiry that PHCoE asked us to address, we conducted a programmatic review of four well-established IOPs. To support its response to Congress, PHCoE was interested in understanding the different program components available to active-duty service members. This review also provides context for the policy review detailed in Chapter Four. With the help of our PHCoE and TRICARE points of contact for the FY 2019 NDAA's Section 702 pilot study, we worked to identify direct-care and private-sector IOPs to use as case illustrations, starting with a list of 205 IOPs provided by TRICARE.[1] We also conducted exploratory searches of select websites with search engines designed to identify mental health treatment facilities.

None of the search engines were comprehensive enough to identify the totality of IOPs serving service members suffering from the psychological aftermath of sexual assault in the military.[2]

We selected two private-sector programs and two operated by DoD for our review and held discussions with select IOP administrators and clinicians who described the IOP programs, practices, and variation in pro-

---

[1] We purposefully did not hold discussions with IOPs in the Sexual Trauma Intensive Outpatient Program TRICARE pilot study because they were already being evaluated.

[2] Our methods for identifying and selecting programs are detailed in Appendix B. We attempted to identify programs with a PTSD IOP that have at least two patient tracks, one for the treatment of sexual trauma and one for the treatment of combat-related trauma. That step enabled us to understand whether IOPs for PTSD could meet the needs of service members suffering from different types of trauma.

gram components and approaches. We selected programs that treat a larger number of patients, have been in existence for several years, and were known to some military mental health providers, for the purposes of including programs that used evidence-based treatments and that may have data on relevant health outcomes. We conducted online searches for programs that would allow us to compare services for sexual assault-related PTSD relative to other PTSD at a DoD IOP and a private-sector IOP.

Attempts were also made to identify IOPs located in known areas of need identified by TRICARE points of contact, specifically in the Fayetteville, North Carolina area, San Antonio, Texas, and the Pacific Northwest around Joint Base Lewis-McCord; considerations were also made to reach out to private-sector IOPs located within a reasonable distance from military installations. Using these strategies, we selected for inclusion four programs representing examples of programs available to service members and veterans.

Outreach included team members either emailing or calling program points of contact. We contacted 15 organizations with IOPs, 11 of which were operating in the private sector, two programs within the VA, and two programs within DoD. Several of these outreach discussions revealed additional insights that may be of interest to DHA program administrators or network administrators.

We spoke to a total of 18 individuals involved in business operations, clinical care, and program leadership.[3] In this chapter, we summarize the information gained from these discussions for the four case illustrations. We describe the history and administration of the programs, review the main components of program design and treatment, and describe information we collected on outcomes and effects of the program for active-duty service members. We also present observations from clinical program directors and additional insights gained during the initial period of program outreach as part of our case study selection process. Because we spoke only to clinicians and administrators from facilities with successful IOPs that receive active-duty service members, their comments to us appeared expectedly biased in favor of such programs.

---

[3] See Appendix A for a discussion guide we developed to cover specific topics with different types of program staff.

Intensive Outpatient Reviews

We held discussions with program staff and reviewed program material from four IOPs to document program characteristics and experiences. Each program differs in important ways. One private-sector program (Comprehensive Wellness Center [CWC]) treats a predominantly dually diagnosed population (typically substance abuse and PTSD) and is funded through patients using private insurance and TRICARE. The second program (UCF Restores at the University of Central Florida) is grant-funded and resides outside the MHS and TRICARE network. Two programs are housed in MTFs; a trauma processing group (Evolution) and one that treats sexual trauma in a separate track using individual therapy (Walter Reed National Military Medical Center). We do not present the case illustrations as best practices nor as illustrative of an "average IOP," if such a characterization exists. Instead, these programs illuminate the diversity of options among IOPs and describe the specific experiences and opinions of a handful of clinicians and administrators.

Using these conversations, we learned about a variety of program types and treatment components, where the programs align, and how they differ. Across these IOPs we found that the types of treatment offered to treat sexual trauma varied, and this is summarized in Table 3.1. No single treatment type was used across all four programs, but those consistent with recommended treatments in the VA/DoD clinical practice guidelines for PTSD, CBT, and EMDR were used in three of the four programs (VA and DoD, 2017). UCF Restores and Evolution are very specific about their core treatment types, although Evolution offers more adjunctive therapy options. With the exception of UCF Restores, the programs offer other components such as yoga, art therapy, mindfulness, nutritional assessment, and sleep hygiene.

In addition, the structure of the programs varied greatly, as outlined in Table 3.2. UCF Restores and the Evolution programs have cohort admissions and specify exact program length: 15 days and 5 weeks, respectively. The other two programs, CWC and Walter Reed, offer more flexible timelines (although Walter Reed's program is about four weeks long and CWC's average length is about the same), rolling admissions, and an array of treatment options. All programs treat both men and women, and officers and enlisted.

TABLE 3.1

Programs and Treatment Types

| | Private Sector | | DoD | |
	CWC	UCF Restores	Evolution Trauma IOP	Walter Reed IOP
Accelerated resolution therapy				X
CBT	X	X		X
CPT			X	X
Dialectical behavior therapy (DBT)	X			
EMDR	X		X	X
Medication-assisted treatment	X			
PE			X	X
Reconsolidation of traumatic memories	X			
Trauma-management therapy (TMT)		X		
Written exposure therapy				X

All of the programs offer mixed gender sessions, and, of the three programs that discussed mixing officers and enlisted service members, Evolution said mixing is avoided, if possible, while the two private-sector IOPs do mix the groups (although CWC noted it has only ever had one officer). Programs that segment groups do so to build group cohesion and create a level of comfort to make it easier for individuals to talk about difficult subjects.[4]

The case descriptions of the history, administration, and design of the IOPs reveal the variation among them. Although the variation might make it difficult to directly compare the programs, it illustrates the benefit of having different treatment approaches that can be tailored to the needs

---

[4] Discussion with Tracy Jones-Williams, April 27, 2021.

TABLE 3.2

Program Structure for Treating Trauma

	Private Sector		DoD	
	CWC	UCF Restores	Evolution Trauma IOP	Walter Reed IOP
Enrollment type (cohort/rolling)	Rolling	Cohort	Cohort	Rolling
Length of program	Flexible	15 days	5 weeks	~4 weeks
Enlisted and officers same session (Y/N)	Y	Y	Avoid if possible	—
Mixed gender sessions offered (Y/N)	Y	Y	Y	Y

of individual patients. The existence of these programs and their apparent success are evidence that it is possible to treat service members with PTSD resulting from sexual assault in an IOP, either on a military installation or in the private sector. We now turn to each case study in turn.

Case 1: CWC

CWC opened in late 2015. Andrew Baker, clinical director at CWC, joined the following year.[5] The priority at the outset was to gain accreditation from the Joint Commission. At that time, because of the nature of the industry, virtually no insurer would reimburse a facility without accreditation, and accreditation needed to be in place before CWC could conduct business.[6] In early 2021, the patient population of CWC was approximately 30 percent to 35 percent active-duty military, veteran, or dependents.[7]

The facility offers care at every level: inpatient, PHP, IOP, and outpatient. Most clients enter CWC at the inpatient level and step down to PHP after about one to two weeks. The usual length of stay at the PHP level is 30 days, after which clients will step down to the IOP, usually to IOP 6 (six days a

---

[5] Discussion with Andrew Baker, April 9, 2021.

[6] Discussion with Andrew Baker, April 9, 2021.

[7] Discussion with Jonathan Smith, March 25, 2021.

week), where they tend to spend a week or two. Clients can step down to IOP 3 (three days a week), which usually lasts about a month but can take as long as six months, and then patients finally step down to outpatient treatment.[8] Only about one person a month will enter at the IOP level.[9]

The overarching philosophy of CWC is to focus on flexibility and individual needs. The individual treatment options are varied and include EMDR, DBT, CBT, reconciliation of traumatic memories, and medication-assisted treatment.[10] CWC also offers clients a wide array of other components of which they can choose to take advantage, including massage therapy, meditation, art therapy, physical therapy, holistic therapy, music therapy, chiropractic care, brain mapping, pharmacogenetic testing, nutritional assessments and counseling, case management, lab tests and screenings, neurotherapy, family therapy and education, trauma conscious yoga, and equine therapy. As CWC's Baker explained, they are willing to offer anything that is supported by research and if they do not have it, CWC will try to help people access it. There is also a large emphasis on engaging with the patient's family and support system.[11]

Both PHP and IOP levels of care have three treatment tracks: substance abuse, mental health, and trauma. Most patients are dual diagnosis, meaning there is some level of substance abuse treatment in all tracks. The substance abuse track, which is based on the 12-step program (Nowinski, Baker, and Carroll, 1999), is only about two to three weeks. The other tracks are open-ended, and people may attend the substance abuse track prior to one of the other two.

When COVID-19 restrictions began, CWC introduced hybrid programming. Many of the patients lived onsite and in-person meetings were maintained, although with social distancing and masks required. Off-site participants joined in via Zoom. Because of its sensitive nature, trauma therapy was required to be in-person.[12]

---

[8] Discussion with Andrew Baker, April 9, 2021.

[9] Discussion with Kimberleigh Stickney, April 7, 2021.

[10] Appendix C contains brief descriptions of these treatment approaches.

[11] Discussion with Andrew Baker, April 9, 2021.

[12] Discussion with Kimberleigh Stickney, April 7, 2021.

In terms of outcome measurement, CWC's Baker said that the problem with many outcome measures is they are focused on short-term symptom reduction or binary outcomes such as whether someone remains sober or not. In reality, second and third order changes (like relationship quality or job performance), which are harder to both achieve and measure, should be the goals.[13] As Baker explained, some patients have been to a large number of treatment facilities—and, although these patients probably will not achieve full, long-term sobriety, they can still positively affect their lives and longevity. He was referencing the entire patient population at CWC, not describing a typical service member experience.

Kimberleigh Stickney, military and veteran coordinator, military liaison, and trauma therapist at CWC, noted a service member's relationship with the military often changes in dramatic ways following experiences of sexual or combat trauma. She explained that many different types of steps and phases accompany the healing process. CWC has patients whom the center is trying to return to duty and others whom it is helping through the medical board process and the transition back to civilian life, including helping the patients pursue educational benefits.[14] Indeed, many of the individuals we spoke to noted that a significant proportion of patients are going through the disability evaluation process, referred to as the *medical board process*. Stickney emphasized the importance of individualized care as CWC assists patients come to terms with their relationship with the military. She observed that this process is especially sensitive for patients who experienced sexual trauma but have not yet been able to process their anger toward the military.

Despite the reported challenges in quantifying and measuring certain treatment outcomes, CWC administers several clinical measures on a monthly basis for their military patients, including the PTSD Checklist for DSM-5 (PCL-5), Brief Addiction Monitor-Revised (BAM-R), Generalized Anxiety Disorder-7 (GAD-7) scale, and the PHQ-9.[15] The clinicians use these data in conjunction with clinical interviewing and clinical judg-

---

[13] Discussion with Andrew Baker, April 9, 2021.

[14] Discussion with Kimberleigh Stickney, April 7, 2021.

[15] Discussion with Kimberleigh Stickney, April 7, 2021.

ment to help determine who will be placed in the different treatment tracks and to help monitor the effects of, and concurrently inform, care delivery.[16] In addition, CWC collects data about rates of discharge types. According to data provided by staff, 22 percent of all patients successfully completed treatment, 11 percent completed an episode of care in which they maintain sobriety for 30 days, 18 percent were referred to an outside agency, 2 percent completed the IOP but left before completing outpatient treatment, 5 percent underwent administrative discharge initiated by CWC, 23 percent left voluntarily before completing treatment against staff advice, 14 percent did not have applicable data available, and 5 percent had some other discharge type (i.e., left involuntarily, noncompliant). The staff did not report data separately for service member patients.

Patients must sign a release of information form that allows CWC to send a weekly update report to the referring provider from the patient's military base, including urinalysis and Breathalyzer results and progress notes.[17] Stickney indicated that active-duty patients return to outpatient care with their previous providers at the MTF, noting that the patients are typically required to meet with their providers for a minimum of one session per month following discharge, even if they are in the medical board process.[18]

Case 2: UCF Restores IOP

Established in 2011, the UCF Restores IOP was created by Executive Director Deborah Beidel and is run in coordination with Amie Newins of the Rosengren Trauma Clinic, which is associated with the University of Central Florida. The clinic also includes an outpatient program and a single-session consultation program (UCF Restores, undated).[19] The UCF Restores IOP aims to treat trauma and return patients to military service as quickly

---

[16] Discussion with Andrew Baker, April 9, 2021. See also Appendix D for descriptions of these measures.

[17] Discussion with Kimberleigh Stickney, April 7, 2021; emails from Lisa di Fiori, August 5–6, 2021.

[18] Discussion with Kimberleigh Stickney, April 7, 2021.

[19] Data provided in email from Amie Newins, April 27, 2021.

as possible by conducting a three-week program using TMT.[20] This type of therapy consists of exposure therapy sessions using virtual reality and group therapy sessions, addressing such topics as fear, anxiety, depression, and social isolation (CWC, 2020). As Beidel, Stout, et al., 2017, noted (p. 110):

> TMT is a multicomponent behavioral treatment program designed to target the multidimensional nature of combat-related PTSD: reducing emotional and physiological reactivity to traumatic cues, reducing intrusive symptoms and avoidance behavior, improving interpersonal skills and emotion modulation (e.g., anger control), improving sleep, and increasing the range of enjoyable social activities. TMT consists of several interrelated components: education, intensive exposure, social and emotional rehabilitation, homework assignments, flexibility exercises, and programmed practice.

In a discussion with us, Beidel said that although exposure therapy is "hard and nasty," it is extremely powerful for reducing PTSD symptoms. Whereas other programs try to match the virtual reality exposure as closely as possible to the true experience, Beidel said this factor can actually be a distraction. UCF Restores does not attempt this experience, and the program does not believe this has a negative effect on treatment outcomes because program officials have seen considerable reduction in Clinician-Administered PTSD Scale for DSM-5 (CAPS-5) scores.[21]

At the clinic in Florida, individuals are enrolled into the program on a cohort basis, at no cost to patients because the IOP is funded through research grants funding studies on various components of their IOP.[22] The program is not part of the TRICARE network; it is governed by the regulations of the university and the state of Florida.[23] The program participants include active-duty service members, which so far have made up approximately 15 percent of participants, veterans (30 percent), first responders

---

[20] Discussion with Amie Newins, April 6, 2021.

[21] Discussion with Deborah Beidel, March 16, 2021.

[22] Data provided in email from Amie Newins, April 27, 2021.

[23] Discussion with Monica Potts, April 13, 2021.

(46 percent), and civilians (9 percent).[24] To date, the majority of patients who have experienced sexual trauma during their time in the military are women. According to the clinical case coordinator, active-duty service members participate in the program from out of state through temporary duty (TDY), with lodging paid by their command. In addition, some local service members have been able to attend. It was stated that sometimes TDY requirements can be a barrier to quick enrollment.[25] This may not be surprising given it takes detailed coordination between the MTF, the civilian treatment facility, and the service member's command.

During COVID-19–related restrictions, operations were conducted virtually using telehealth; in-person treatment resumed in February 2021, with lodging and some meals provided for participants at a nearby hotel. When the program was conducted via telehealth, virtual reality was not used because they do not have remote systems or equipment that could be sent to patients.[26]

Cohorts enter the program once a month with a maximum of eight participants and an average of four to six.[27] Sessions over the three weeks consist of 2.5 to five hours per day with a total of at least 29 sessions (15 imaginal exposure sessions and 14 skills-based group sessions) run by trained staff, some of whom are veterans, and one clinician per one to two patients, who stay with those patients for the entire program. Participants are combined regardless of rank or gender; considerations are made to ensure that female service members are comfortable with all-male groups.[28]

Program staff collect a variety of data to help guide care delivery and to document treatment outcomes for research, beginning with a telephone screening conducted by Monica Potts, clinical case coordinator at UCF Restores, to assess for program fit. Potts collects demographic information, focuses on the presence and severity of trauma and depressive symptoms,

---

[24] Data provided in email from Amie Newins, April 27, 2021.

[25] Data provided in email from Amie Newins, April 27, 2021.

[26] Email from Amie Newins, August 4, 2021.

[27] Discussion with Amie Newins, April 6, 2021.

[28] Discussion with Monica Potts, April 13, 2021; discussion with Amie Newins, April 6, 2021; and data provided in email from Amie Newins, April 27, 2021.

the degree to which symptoms permeate throughout an individual's life, and assesses for the presence of substance abuse that may require detoxification prior to program entry.[29] She also collects a treatment history and conducts a risk assessment for threats of harm to self or another.[30] Potts then educates the prospective patient about the differences between outpatient care and an IOP.[31] She emphasizes the three-week duration of IOP if she believes that the individual will be better served by this more-intensive therapy.[32]

Following confirmed eligibility for the program, but prior to beginning treatment, a clinician conducts a formal intake assessment, beginning with a past month version of the CAPS-5 and the Anxiety and Related Disorders Interview Schedule for DSM-5 (ADIS-5) to assess whether the patient meets diagnostic criteria for PTSD, or if they have other symptoms that can be treated through the program.[33] The past week version of the CAPS-5 is administered by the patient's clinician immediately prior to discharge and at three and six months post-intake. The Life Events Checklist for DSM-5 (LEC-5) is also collected at intake, and the following self-report measures are collected at intake, each Monday of the IOP, and at three and six months post-intake: PCL- 5, PHQ-9, GAD-7, Dimension of Anger-5 (DAR-5), Alcohol Use Disorders Identification Test (AUDIT), Cannabis Use Disorders Identification Test-Revised (CUDIT-R), and the Drug Abuse Screening Test-10 (DAST-10).

In addition, clinicians routinely employ therapy assignments, worksheets, and activity and sleep monitoring logs to be completed outside therapy sessions. Lastly, each clinician completes a clinician checklist at the beginning of every individual therapy appointment following the intake, which briefly assesses the patient's general level of distress, the experience of any traumatic events since the prior session, amount of alcohol consumed

---

[29] Discussion with Monica Potts, April 13, 2021.

[30] Discussion with Monica Potts, April 13, 2021.

[31] Discussion with Monica Potts, April 13, 2021.

[32] Discussion with Monica Potts, April 13, 2021.

[33] See Appendix D for descriptions of these measurement tools.

since the prior session, the presence of any angry/aggressive outbursts, and safety risks.[34]

The completion rate of the program is 98 percent, and treatment gains in patients with combat-related PTSD have been well documented (Beidel, Stout, et al., 2017; Beidel, Frueh, et al., 2017).[35] Potts highlighted the positive effect on participants, saying, "Most of them no longer meet diagnostic criteria post [treatment], they are in a place where they can function normally, and their recovery can continue. Patients will refer other participants; this speaks for itself for how impactful the IOP program is." In addition to the individual therapy sessions and group skills, having a cohesive group where participants could support each other was critical. Beidel acknowledged that UCF Restores does not yet know the impact of patients staying at the same hotel for the duration of the program, compared with IOPs in which patients return home each night after the day's session, but emphasized that the group cohesion was very important.[36]

Potts described how she approaches post-program treatment planning with her active-duty patients. Potts meets with her patients at the end of the program period to collaboratively discuss their needs and to offer clinical recommendations. She explained that active-duty patients typically have a behavioral health provider on base which helps facilitate continuity of care back into an outpatient setting. If a service member is involved in the medical board process, Potts will assemble a list of resources to help the patient find a new provider near where they will be living. As with all her patients, Potts conducts a final assessment of PTSD symptoms using the CAPS-5 to understand how they have responded to treatment. The assessment battery also includes self-report measures of anxiety, depression, substance use, and anger, for example, which the clinicians are able to compare to the same measures collected during the intake session. The scores are used to help guide discussions around post-treatment planning.[37]

---

[34] Data provided in email by Monica Potts, April 22, 2021.

[35] Data also provided in email from Amie Newins, April 27, 2021.

[36] Discussion with Deborah Beidel, March 16, 2021.

[37] Discussion with Monica Potts, April 13, 2021.

We learned that the UCF Restores program will evaluate a two-week condensed version of the IOP compared with the current three-week version, which would make for a more time- and cost- effective program if found to have equivalent effects, and may be more feasible, especially for active-duty service members.[38] Planned research also includes evaluating the efficacy of the IOP specifically for the treatment of sexual trauma, while $10 million in funding from the U.S. Army in 2018 is allowing Restores to replicate the program in three locations serving active-duty service members in the Army, Navy, and Marine Corps.[39]

Case 3: Evolution Trauma Intensive Outpatient Program

The DoD Evolution Trauma Intensive Outpatient Program, established in 2009, is run out of the U.S. Army's Landstuhl Regional Medical Center in Germany. The Evolution program focuses on treating PTSD in three separate tracks (combat, sexual, and general trauma) using evidence-based methods.[40] The program serves individuals who come from a variety of locations, including active-duty service members in U.S. European Command, U.S. Africa Command, and U.S. Central Command (Landstuhl Regional Medical Center, undated).

Within the Evolution program, a program called Connections to address sexual trauma was started in April 2020 by licensed clinical social worker Tracy Jones-Williams and psychology technician and admissions and referral coordinator Chimnemerem "Chinny" Neal. Connections started as an in-person program that transitioned to virtual treatment because of COVID-19. The Evolutions program is cohort-based; Connections was established on a rolling admissions basis to address the challenges of forming cohorts for program enrollment, in an effort to increase access to care.[41] When there are enough people to form a cohort for the sexual trauma track

---

[38] Discussion with Monica Potts, April 13, 2021.

[39] Discussion with Amie Newins, April 6, 2021. As stated on the program's website, the three locations consist of Dwight D. Eisenhower Army Medical Center, Naval Medical Hospital Portsmouth, and Camp Lejeune (see CWC, 2020).

[40] Discussion with Chimnemerem Neal, April 27, 2021.

[41] Discussion with Tracy Jones-Williams, April 27, 2021.

of treatment, they start that cohort in the Evolutions program. The rolling admissions enrollment method did not exist before Connections. Prior to Connections, only small groups focused on sexual trauma in the IOP.[42] The Evolutions program also has an Evolution Family Support Group, which provides "support and resources in self-care, anger management, communication skills building, and PTSD education to facilitate family members' involvement in the patient's treatment (recovery process)."[43]

A staff clinician indicated that most of the IOP referrals for the Evolution Program come from the Army. The programs serve active-duty service members but also dependents (e.g., spouses) and retirees depending on the space available in the program. At the time of the discussion, there was continued demand for the program with enrollment planned two cohorts ahead. The majority of individuals referred (52 out of 54) were active duty, approximately one-third of whom were already in, or were considering, the medical board process (20 out of 52); clinicians running the Evolution IOP do not affect the medical board process.[44]

To determine Evolutions program eligibility, providers send the referrals to the Evolutions referral coordinator who shares a brochure with program information before meeting with the patient. The intake process reportedly includes a PTSD prognostic evaluation focused on emotional tolerance and motivation for change. Individuals receive acceptance packets that are also seen by their providers. Special attention is given to create group cohesion in cohort assignments by weighing patients' time spent in the service, their military occupational specialty, rank, and index trauma, to ensure service members are comfortable enough to share openly.[45]

Prior to the onset of the COVID-19 pandemic in March 2020, the duration of the Evolutions program was six weeks, with approximately 30 hours a week of treatment using individual and group therapy sessions (Landstuhl Regional Medical Center, undated). The program length was reduced to five weeks during the pandemic and is expected to remain as such moving for-

[42] Discussion with Chimnemerem Neal, April 27, 2021.

[43] Email from Chimnemerem Neal, April 27, 2021.

[44] Discussion with Chimnemerem Neal, April 27, 2021.

[45] Discussion with Chimnemerem Neal, April 27, 2021.

ward.[46] The core of the program revolves around a daily CPT and trauma processing group, which occurs first in the daily schedule at 0800. These sessions are followed by participation in one or more of the 11 different breakout groups that focus on topics and activities such as psychoeducation about exposure principles, interpersonal skill building, emotion regulation, occupational therapy, yoga, music therapy, family and education, and a mindfulness meditation group called "Armor Down."[47] The only group in which patients from different tracks attend in a mixed fashion is the psychoeducation group.

Individual therapy sessions commence in the afternoon, with at least two such sessions per week. Clinicians vary their therapeutic approaches to collaboratively align with patient preferences; EMDR, CPT, DBT, and PE are used most frequently.[48]

Patients complete several measures, such as the PCL-5, GAD-7, PHQ-9, and the Columbia-Suicide Severity Rating Scale (C-SSRS), during the intake assessment and then weekly while in the program. Clinicians use the scores to monitor treatment progress and the staff clinicians noted that although PCL-5 scores typically increase during week two of the program as trauma accounts begin to be discussed in greater detail, symptoms begin to abate in week three and decrease overall compared with baseline by completion of the program.[49] Staff clinicians reported that participants rarely drop out of the Evolutions program.[50]

Case 4: Walter Reed National Military Medical Center Psychiatry Continuity Service IOP

Walter Reed National Military Medical Center has long had a trauma recovery (mostly combat trauma) IOP and a general mental health IOP, and both are part of its *comprehensive recovery track*. Clinicians at Walter Reed found

---

[46] Discussion with Chimnemerem Neal, April 27, 2021.

[47] Discussion with Tracy Jones-Williams, April 27, 2021.

[48] Discussion with Tracy Jones-Williams, April 27, 2021.

[49] Discussion with Tracy Jones-Williams, April 27, 2021.

[50] Discussion with Tracy Jones-Williams, April 27, 2021.

that putting individuals with sexual trauma in the general trauma track went poorly because of differences in emotional expression, content, and methods of processing between patients with a history of combat versus sexual trauma. Clinicians observed that these features can be triggering for patients in mixed-trauma group settings. Therefore, a pilot program was initiated in 2014 with a separate weekly sexual trauma group, called the interpersonal recovery track, and it has been ongoing since then.

Walter Reed also offers a PHP. It does not have outpatient treatment options and are not an entry level of care; most people enter the IOP as a step up from outpatient treatment or step down from inpatient treatment in other programs. The IOP used a cohort admissions system for many years, but eventually, as the waitlist grew, they switched to rolling admissions, against the wishes of the clinicians, who appreciated the trust-building elements of the cohort model.[51] Referrals into the IOP primarily come from the Walter Reed National Military Medical Center region, but have also included patients from the West Coast and patients who are stepping down from inpatient care after having been medically evacuated from Germany, Kuwait, and Qatar for behavioral health reasons.[52]

The program, which lasts about one month, consists of three groups a day, which may consist of DBT, CBT, or CPT. In individual therapy, clinicians rely on a variety of approaches, selecting the treatment that best aligns with a patient's presentation and preferences: PE, written exposure, CPT, accelerated resolution therapy, and EMDR. The program also offers adjunctive therapies, such as art therapy, community integration, recreational therapy, and transcranial magnetic stimulation (on an as needed basis), to enhance the effectiveness of the primary evidence-based treatments for PTSD. When COVID-19 began in early 2020, the IOPs went "mostly virtual."[53]

The program benefits from such resources as wraparound services and the collective expertise of a diverse network of providers whose breadth of training backgrounds ensures that patients' needs are met. Additional strengths include utilization of the centralized electronic medical record

---

[51] Discussion with Kerrie Earley, April 14, 2021.

[52] Discussion with Kerrie Earley, April 14, 2021.

[53] Discussion with Kerrie Earley, April 14, 2021.

(Armed Forces Health Longitudinal Technology Application [AHLTA] system), which helps facilitate communication with referring providers throughout treatment and upon discharge when patients are referred back for outpatient follow-up care. We did not discuss the utilization of the Behavioral Health Data Portal (BHDP) by Evolution staff. A staff clinician emphasized that these strengths, along with the voluntary nature of the program and the potential for stepped up and stepped down care, contribute to the very rare instance in which a patient does not complete the program.[54]

Clinical Program Directors' Observations

We sought to understand potential rationales for using IOPs as opposed to outpatient care, and we spoke with those who design and implement the programs, and who have built in positive biases toward the value of IOPs. Our discussions with clinical directors revealed insights and hypotheses about the IOP model of treatment and the important components of care. Beidel addressed differences in attrition rates in different types of programs, describing the high attrition in outpatient trauma-focused treatment compared with the very low attrition rates in IOPs.[55] As Newins explained, the condensed timeline of the IOP helps "avoids stigma and helps people get better faster, which also helps people stay in treatment. Even by the end of the week, people start to feel better, so we don't have the drop out problems that typical PTSD programs have with this shorter timeline."[56] These perspectives are supported in research which has shown that trauma exposure-based treatments have high rates of dropout (Edwards-Stewart et al., 2021) and that IOPs for PTSD have very low dropout rates (Ragsdale et al., 2020).

In terms of whether to hold mixed trauma groups or cohorts, Army COL Wendi Waits, a psychiatrist and director of behavioral health at Walter Reed National Military Medical Center, thought it was clinically appropriate to treat active-duty service members with trauma due to sexual assault

---

[54] Discussion with Kerrie Earley, April 14, 2021.

[55] Discussion with Deborah Beidel, March 16, 2021.

[56] Discussion with Amie Newins, April 6, 2021.

in the military in groups with civilians with PTSD following sexual trauma.[57] She thought the clinical themes and the desire to find empowerment and strength and to forget the traumatic experience(s) would be similar for military and civilian female populations. Waits described the clinical themes attached to treatment of combat trauma differently; for example, often active-duty service members want to hold on to the memory out of respect for those who may have been injured and killed. She suggested that the moral injury associated with combat trauma calls for different clinical content.

Relatedly, CWC's Baker said, "pain is pain," and suggested there may be value in groups that include people with different types of traumas, because it could be "normalizing," and all patients have a common goal of "getting their lives back on track, that's what ties them together." Air Force CMSgt (ret.) Andrew Laning, the Universal Health Services (UHS) divisional director of military programs, said he thought that the main benefit of these IOPs was allowing active-duty members to enter into a support group and to feel accepted.[58]

In regard to the IOP model, Waits wondered whether reacculturation after completing a private-sector IOP is an issue (e.g., does communication with chain of command become less formal?). She also addressed the challenges associated with COVID-19; DoD computers cannot use Skype, and patient symptom acuity is harder to recognize and manage via telemedicine platforms.

In the next chapter we turn to a different, but related topic, that of policies governing these programs and service member access.

---

[57] Discussion with Wendi Waits, April 7, 2021.

[58] Discussion with Air Force CMSgt (ret.) Andrew Laning II, April 22, 2021.

CHAPTER FOUR

Policies Governing IOPs

We also reviewed DoD policies that define the requirements for a TRICARE-funded or MHS IOP and that govern clinical management of active-duty service members—PHCoE's third topic of interest. The discussions we held with IOP administrators and care coordinators helped us understand how these policies are implemented. The information shared during these discussions support the possibility of including IOPs outside the MHS to treat service members and, in some instances, make the case for why access to those providers could be beneficial. In this chapter we begin with an overview of current health care provisions for active-duty service members and the types of policies reviewed. We then explore four policy areas applicable to IOPs: approval processes, payment policies, program access, and clinical management.

Overview of Current Health Care Provisions

As a brief background, the MHS provides health care for active-duty service members, their dependents, and retirees. The cornerstone of the MHS is direct care provided at MTFs. Through the TRICARE network, the MHS supplements direct care with the private sector at civilian facilities and, when necessary, at VHA facilities. Active-duty service members are eligible for TRICARE Prime, which is designed like an "HMO [health maintenance organization] with primary and specialty care from military or contracted civilian providers" and no cost-sharing for enrolled members for services in the TRICARE network (Tanielian and Farmer, 2019).

DoD operates 721 MTFs at military bases and posts around the world (Mendez, 2020b). These facilities include large medical centers with inpatient and outpatient services and multiple subspecialties, hospitals that also offer hospitalization and outpatient services and specialties, and clinics with only outpatient services (TRICARE, undated-b; TRICARE, 2021a).

The MHS supplements the MTFs' "capabilities with care purchased from the private sector through provider networks established and managed by contractors known as third-party administrators," which are currently Humana Military and Health Net Federal Services (Tanielian and Farmer, 2019).

It is important to be aware that the VHA also operates a variety of inpatient and outpatient facilities of varying sizes and specialties.[1] The authority for VHA and DOD to enter into partnerships and agreements for the sharing of resources is provided in 38 U.S.C. 8111. It authorizes them to "enter into agreements and contracts for the mutually beneficial coordination, use, or exchange of use of the VA and DoD health care resources with the goal of improving the access to, and quality and cost effectiveness of, the health care provided by Veterans Health Administration and the Military Health System to the beneficiaries of both departments."

VA medical facilities may join TRICARE provider networks and treat TRICARE beneficiaries, including active-duty service members (DoDI 6010.23, 2020; VHA Handbook 1660.04, 2015; VHA Directive 1660.06, 2019). A 2002 memorandum of understanding between the VA and DoD outlines the "general requirements for agreements between a DoD regional managed care support contractor (MCS) and a VA health care facility under which the managed care support contractor may include the facility in the contractor's networks" (TRICARE Policy Manual 6010.54-M, Chapter 11, Section 2.1, 2002, p. 3). Under such agreements, VA medical facilities negotiate rates directly with the MSC contractors and are "subject to the same utilization management and quality assurance requirements applicable to other network providers" (DoDI 6010.23, 2020). Within the VHA, there is substantial encouragement for facilities, particularly "very large community-based outpatient clinics," to open IOPs (VHA Handbook

---

[1] We did not analyze VA policies as many of the important policy documents are not publicly accessible. We held initial discussions with VA psychologists but did not review any VA IOPs.

1160.01, 2008). This agreement expands the treatment options potentially available to active-duty service members and veterans.

Types of Policies Reviewed

The policies we reviewed pertained primarily to substance use disorder and mental health IOPs. We were interested in the approval process, payment policies, policies for accessing IOPs, and clinical management policies. We reviewed approximately 90 documents, primarily including policy manuals, instructions, orders, and relevant federal regulations (see Table 4.1 for key policy areas and pertinent policies). As the main military health care provider and insurance network, TRICARE manuals were most relevant in the documentation of policies relating to the approval process and payments in private-sector facilities.

Some documents were obtained through internet-based searches of the TRICARE network contractors' websites Humana and Health Net, in addition to some that were provided by PHCoE and TRICARE points of contact. In regard to private-sector care, the primary policy documents reviewed were the TRICARE Policy Manual, Reimbursement Manual, Operations Manual, and Code of Federal Regulations (CFR).[2] We relied on other documents, such as various guidance documents and handbooks published by the TRICARE contractors, Health Net Federal Services, and Humana, when relevant. We reviewed DoD Instructions (DoDIs), some service-level policies, and manuals for medical providers pertaining to clinical treatment guidance. Finally, we reviewed information published by the accreditation organizations, the Joint Commission, the Council on Accreditation (COA), and the Commission on Accreditation of Rehabilitation Facilities (CARF) (Joint Commission, undated-a; Council on Accreditation, undated-a; CARF, undated-a). Although an active-duty service member may also receive treatment from VHA facilities, we focused on MHS and private-sector facilities in this report.

---

[2] Specifically, we reviewed 32 CFR 199, 1986, which covers Civilian Health and Medical Program of the Uniformed Services (CHAMPUS). CHAMPUS is the previous name for TRICARE.

TABLE 4.1

Policy Guidance for IOPs for Service Members

Policy Area	Policy
Approval policies	
Accreditation of DoD IOPs	DHA Procedures Manual 6025.13, Vol. 5
Licensing and credentialing of DoD MTF practitioners	DoDM 6025.13, 2020; DHA Procedures Manual 6025.13, Vol. 4
Authorization, accreditation and licensing of private-sector IOPs	TRICARE Policy Manual 6010.60-M, Chapter 11, Section 2.7
Licensing and credentialing of private-sector practitioners	TRICARE Policy Manual 6010.60-M, Chapter 11, Section 3.2
Payment policies	
Reimbursement for per diem for private-sector IOPs	32 CFR 199.14; TRICARE Reimbursement Manual, Chapter 13, Section 2
Policies for accessing an IOP	
Referring service members to an IOP	TRICARE Policy Manual 6010.61-M, Chapter 7, Section 3.5
Placing service members on temporary duty orders	Joint Travel Regulations, Chapter 3, Part D, Par. 0330
Reimbursement for transportation to IOP in local area	TRICARE Reimbursement Manual 6010.61-M, Chapter 7, Section 2; Joint Travel Regulations, Appendix B
Reimbursement for transportation and lodging for IOP that requires overnight stay	Joint Travel Regulations, Chapter 3, Part D, Par. 0330 (DoD, 2022c)
Select clinical management policies	
Problematic substance use guidance	DoDI 1010.04; Secretary of the Navy Instruction (SECNAVINST) 5300.28; AFI 44-121
HIPAA guidelines for DoD health programs	DoDI 6025.18
Individual medical readiness requirements	DoDI 6025.19

Table 4.1—Continued

Policy Area	Policy
Deployment-limiting medical conditions for service members	DoDI 6490.07
Command notification requirements for mental health care	DoDI 6490.08; Army Directive 2020-13
Medical record charting guidance	TRICARE Policy Manual 6010.60-M, Chapter 1, Section 5.1

NOTE: CFR = Code of Federal Regulations.

Approval Processes for IOPs

Active-duty service members may receive treatment through an IOP at either DoD MTFs or in the private sector, either in a hospital setting or a freestanding IOP (TRICARE Policy Manual 6010.60-M, Chapter 11, Section 2.7, 2017). Those IOPs must be accredited, licensed, and credentialed to accept patients. The process for the approval of an IOP at an MTF is less onerous than for a private-sector facility in the TRICARE network.

DoD IOPs

All DoD MTFs must be accredited by an approved external accrediting organization (DHA Procedures Manual 6025.13, Vol. 5, 2019b). IOPs at Army MTFs are accredited by the Joint Commission, which is a nonprofit organization that accredits and certifies health care organizations in the United States, the largest of its kind (Joint Commission, undated-b; Joint Commission, undated-c). Navy MTFs are also accredited by the Joint Commission (Bureau of Medicine and Surgery Instruction 6000.2F, 2017). In the Air Force, all outpatient MTFs are accredited by the Accreditation Association for Ambulatory Health Care (AFI 44-119, 2007).

DoD also requires that all health care practitioners at MTFs be licensed by the relevant jurisdiction and credentialed (DHA Procedures Manual 6025.13, Vol. 4, 2019a). The specific requirements for credentialing consist of a qualifying educational degree; postgraduate training certificate; current professional registrations, licenses, and certifications; experience and any gaps in service going back ten years; malpractice information; evidence of a criminal background check; and proof of professional competence (DHA Procedures Manual 6025.13, Vol. 4, 2019a).

Private-Sector IOPs

IOPs in the private sector may be part of either hospital or freestanding facilities. Approvals for IOPs that are situated in hospitals have a less burdensome approval process because the IOP is automatically approved if the hospital is TRICARE-approved. There is no separate authorization process (32 CFR 199.6; TRICARE Policy Manual 6010.60-M, Chapter 11, Section 2.7, 2017). Approval of freestanding IOPs for treatment of active-duty service members has several important components, including, at the top line, authorization, certification, and credentialing review (see Figure 4.1).[3]

Authorization

The first aspect is *authorization*. All freestanding IOPs must enter into a participation agreement with the DHA director or their designee (TRICARE Policy Manual 6010.60-M, Chapter 11, Section 2.7, 2017; TRICARE Policy Manual 6010.60-M, Chapter 11, Addendum G, 2017). An inspec-

FIGURE 4.1

Approval Process for Private-Sector IOPs

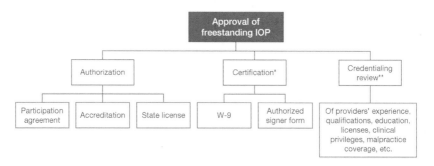

NOTE: * From Humana IOP Certification Form, which also includes all authorization elements.
** Required by Humana and Health Net.

---

[3] The TRICARE Policy Manual and regional contractors use slightly different terminology and categorization. We rely on the TRICARE Policy Manual except where specified.

tion by DHA personnel may be required before signing. The participation agreement also requires the following of the IOP (TRICARE Policy Manual 6010.60-M, Chapter 11, Section 2.7, 2017):

- Render intensive outpatient program services to eligible TRI-CARE beneficiaries in need of such services, in accordance with the participation agreement and TRICARE regulation.
- Accept payment for its services based upon the methodology provided in § 199.14, or such other method as determined by the Director; . . .
- (6) Submit claims for services provided to TRICARE beneficiaries at least every 30 days (except to the extent a delay is necessitated by efforts to first collect from other health insurance). If claims are not submitted at least every 30 days, the IOP agrees not to bill the beneficiary or the beneficiary's family for any amounts disallowed by TRICARE;
- Free-standing intensive outpatient programs shall certify that:
    (i) It is and will remain in compliance with the provisions of paragraph (b)(4)(xii) of this section establishing standards for psychiatric and substance use disorder (SUD) IOPs;
    (ii) It has conducted a self-assessment of the facility's compliance with the [TRICARE] Standards for Intensive Outpatient Programs, as issued by the DHA, Director, and notified the Director of any matter regarding which the facility is not in compliance with such standards; and
    (iii) It will maintain compliance with the TRICARE standards for IOPs, as issued by the Director, except for any such standards regarding which the facility notifies the Director, or a designee that it is not in compliance.
- Designate an individual who will act as liaison for TRICARE inquiries. The IOP shall inform TRICARE, or a designee in writing of the designated individual;
- Furnish OCHAMPUS with cost data, as requested by OCHAMPUS, certified by an independent accounting firm or other agency as authorized by the Director.
- Comply with all requirements of this section applicable to institutional providers generally concerning accreditation requirements, preauthorization, concurrent care review, claims pro-

cessing, beneficiary liability, double coverage, utilization and
quality review, and other matters;

- Grant the Director, or designee, the right to conduct quality
assurance audits or accounting audits with full access to patients
and records (including records relating to patients who are not
CHAMPUS beneficiaries) to determine the quality and cost
effectiveness of care rendered. The audits may be conducted on a
scheduled or unscheduled (unannounced) basis.

Another major component of authorization is accreditation, which is
also required of DoD facilities. Freestanding IOPs must be accredited by
the Joint Commission, CARF, the COA, or another accrediting organization approved by the DHA director (TRICARE Policy Manual 6010.60-M,
Chapter 11, Section 2.7, 2017). The Joint Commission, CARF, and COA are
all nonprofit organizations that accredit and certify health care providers
according to a detailed set of standards pursuant to a site visit. The term of
accreditation is three, four, and five years, respectively (Joint Commission,
undated-b; CARF, undated-b; COA, undated-b).

The accreditation requirement is not unique to TRICARE. According to
a discussion with Lisa Di Fiori, the director of operations for CWC, it had
been required by most insurers. At that time, in 2016–2017, the industry
had been plagued by bad actors, so insurers began requiring accreditation.
Without Joint Commission accreditation, CWC would not have been able to
conduct business. Now, Di Fiori explained, accreditation is not required by
all insurance companies, but it is still valuable to CWC, particularly because
it is a requirement for the Agency For Health Care Administration certification, which they are now working toward.[4]

Di Fiori also described the Joint Commission accreditation process, both
the initial application process and the renewal process. She explained that
the Joint Commission is about "above and beyond client care," and is "five
steps above" the requirements of the Florida Department of Children and
Families, the state licensing organization. According to the Joint Commission, its accreditation standards "create a culture of excellence based in con-
tinuous process improvement" (Joint Commission, undated-d). With the

---

[4] Discussion with Lisa Di Fiori, April 16, 2021.

initial accreditation, Di Fiori said it is approximately 90 days from application until the inspection team arrives. During that first inspection, the team is on-site for three days. The Joint Commission inspects 1,116 targets, covering client safety, staff safety, environmental control, infection control, and more. After the initial review, the Joint Commission issues a report, and the facility has 30 days to submit its corrective action plan. Time from application to certification could be about four to six months, according to Di Fiori.

The renewal process is largely similar, except that facilities are given a shorter notice about the site visits (which took place on Zoom during COVID-19 restrictions). Upon accreditation, the Joint Commission requires that the facility monitor, track, and analyze a large number of safety and client care factors. For example, Di Fiori said the Joint Commission encouraged CWC to have an employee flu vaccination campaign to boost participation to 80 percent.[5]

For an IOP to be authorized, it must also be licensed by the jurisdiction in which its located, if that jurisdiction licenses IOPs (TRICARE Policy Manual 6010.60-M, Chapter 11, Section 2.7; TRICARE Policy Manual 6010.60-M, Chapter 11, Addendum G, 2017). California, for example, does not license either substance abuse or mental health IOPs (Nelson Hardiman, undated). In 2012, the National Association of State Alcohol and Drug Abuse Directors (NASADAD) reviewed state regulations on substance use disorder programs. At that time, 36 jurisdictions licensed outpatient programs, 29 of which had distinct IOP licensing requirements (NASADAD, 2013, p. 5). Of those, 12 states allowed accreditation from an organization, such as the Joint Commission, COA, or CARF, to substitute for the license (NASADAD, 2013, pp. 19–23).

The Florida state license, issued through the Department of Children and Families is, according to Di Fiori, is "a lot more basic" than the accreditation standards and can miss a lot. A benefit of Joint Commission accreditation is that it allows them to waive the Department of Children and Families license process for three years.[6]

---

[5]   Discussion with Lisa Di Fiori, April 16, 2021.

[6]   Discussion with Lisa Di Fiori, April 16, 2021.

Certification

The second component of the approval process is certification. Humana, the TRICARE East regional contractor, includes the participation agreement, accreditation, and the state license as requirements on the IOP certification form, along with a copy of the W-9 and an authorized signed form (Humana Military, undated-b). In addition to certification, IOPs must comply with additional requirements to be approved for treatment of active-duty service members. In addition to the specifics outlined above, the TRICARE Policy Manual states that IOPs "shall comply with all requirements applicable to institutional providers generally concerning accreditation requirements, concurrent care review, claims processing, beneficiary liability, double coverage, utilization and quality review, and other matters" (TRICARE Policy Manual, 6010.60-M, Chapter 11, Section 2.7, 2017).

In the "Authorization" subsection about IOPs earlier in this chapter, the TRICARE Policy Manual also notes that IOPs must agree to a set of requirements for documentation of treatment in medical records, which includes minimum documentation requirements and the timeline for their incorporation into the medical record (TRICARE Policy Manual, 6010.60-M, Chapter 11, Section 2.7, 2017). In addition, "all services, supplies, equipment, and space necessary to fulfill the requirements of each patient's individualized diagnosis and treatment plan must be included in the reimbursement approved for an authorized IOP" (TRICARE Policy Manual, 6010.60-M, Chapter 11, Section 2.7).

Credentialing Review

The third component of IOP authorization is the *credentialing review*, which is required by the TRICARE regional contractors, Health Net and Humana, to become network providers. The review encompasses providers' experience, qualifications, education, licenses, clinical privileges, malpractice coverage, and more (Health Net Federal Services, 2020, pp. 70–71; Humana, undated). According to federal law, a licensed provider may practice their profession in any jurisdiction of the United States, as long as the practice is within the scope of their authorized federal duties.[7] This law applies to providers who are members of the military services, DoD civilian employees, personal services contractors, and health-care professionals credentialed and privileged at a federal health care facility (DoDM 6025.13, 2020). Facilities with IOPs carry general liability insurance and providers have their own insurance. Medical directors are expected to hold between $1 million and $3 million in insurance claims coverage. Di Fiori explained that they are "kind of mixed together," and costs about $25,000 a year.[8]

Both Humana and Health Net use the Council for Affordable Quality Healthcare Credentialing (CAQH) portal to streamline the submission of materials for credentialing (Health Net Federal Services, 2020, p. 70–71; Humana, undated). Providers submit information once through the CAQH, which is used for all insurers' credential review. Other than the material provided through CAQH, Di Fiori explained that all you do is complete an employee roster and provide social security numbers, license numbers, national provider identifications, and the CAQH IDs. Everything is done electronically on the Humana or Health Net websites, and the only difficulty identified by Di Fiori is that the categorization of facilities in the military does not always match up to what is normally used in the private sector, and CWC initially filed as the wrong type of facility.[9]

Health Net, with its Provider Handbook, provides more information about what the credential review covers (Health Net Federal Services, 2020, p. 71):

- have a signed Medicare CMS-460 Agreement or participate with Medicare on a claim-by-claim basis for eligible Medicare beneficiaries
- provide an SSN for all claims processing; an Employer Identification Number (EIN) may be provided, if group only, but additional information will need to be collected for the required individual criminal background history checks

---

[7] The law is 10 U.S.C. Section 1094(d) as cited in DoD Manual 6025.13, 2020.

[8] See, for example, CWC, 2020; and discussion with Lisa Di Fiori.

[9] Discussion with Lisa Di Fiori, April 16, 2021.

- provide a National Provider Identifier (NPI) for all individuals (Type I) and entities (Type II) billing with your organization
- provide a service that is a covered benefit to the plan member
- agree to conditions of participation per the network agreement
- maintain professional liability coverage in accordance with your provider agreement, but generally the limits are at least $200,000 per occurrence and $600,000 aggregate
- all physicians have active hospital privileges, in good standing, at a Joint Commission or Healthcare Facilities Accreditation Program (HFAP)- accredited facility or Det Norske Vetitas (DNV)- accredited facility (may be waived under specific conditions)
- have a current, valid, unrestricted DEA certificate or State Controlled Substance certificate, if applicable
- have completed education and training appropriate to application specialty(ies)
- have no unexplained gaps in work history for the most recent five years
- have malpractice history not excessive for area and specialty
- have no felony convictions
- have no current Medicare or Medicaid sanctions
- have no current disciplinary actions (including, but not limited to, licensure and hospital privileges) sign and include an unmodified "Credentials Attestation, Authorization and Release"
- provide supporting documentation for all confidential questions on the application.

In addition to the facility and program requirements, individual providers must be licensed or certified in their practice area by the state where the treatment occurs even if the state does not require licensure or certification. A temporary professional state license is sufficient (TRICARE Policy Manual 6010.60-M, Chapter 11, Section 3.2, 2017).

According to Di Fiori, the main challenge of working within the TRICARE network is that the system is overly complex, which means that the CWC employees do not have the ability to address problems as they arise. Di Fiori described a situation in which CWC claims keep being rejected by the system, and, as she explained "we get put into queues where supervisors have 10 days to return our calls. There is no sense of urgency to resolve situations, everything has escalated. . . . We've corresponded for months, and nothing has happened."[10] The Humana Military supervisor whom CWC is currently working with, she explained, is responsible for the 15,000 providers in South Florida and is stretched too thin. She thought that other facilities had stopped accepting TRICARE because of payment issues. With respect to the IOPs, the main problem facing her facility and many others is that TRICARE overpaid them initially because of "system errors" and is now seeking recoupment, which she said can be a significant business hardship.[11]

Payment Policies for IOPs

DoD IOPs

There is no cost-sharing for active-duty service members who obtain treatment at MTFs. At Walter Reed National Medical Center, clinical social worker Kerrie Earley explained that staff code visits in AHLTA, the DoD's global electronic health record system.[12] The delivery of health care at MTFs is funded through the Defense Health Program, which comes from the MHS budget request. The budget request also includes funding for pay and allowances for military medical personnel (Mendez, 2020a).

Private-Sector IOPs

As with the authorization process, hospital-based and freestanding IOPs have different payment policies. Because separate authorization of the IOP is not required, all IOPs in authorized hospitals are automatically eligible for per diem reimbursement under TRICARE's Hospital Outpatient Prospective Payment System (OPPS) (TRICARE Reimbursement Manual 6010.61-M, Chapter 13, Section 2, 2018). TRICARE's OPPS is modeled after the Medicare system and is "based on nationally established Ambulatory Payment Classifications payment amounts and standardized for geographic wage differences that includes operating and capital-related costs that are

---

[10] Discussion with Lisa Di Fiori, April 16, 2021.

[11] Discussion with Lisa Di Fiori, April 16, 2021.

[12] See discussion with Kerrie Earley, April 14, 2021.

directly related and integral to performing a procedure or furnishing a service in a hospital outpatient department" (32 CFR 199.2). The federal regulations make clear that despite attempts to maintain continuity with the Medicare OPPS methodology, deviations may be needed, "to accommodate TRICARE's unique benefit structure and beneficiary population" (32 CFR 199.14 [6][ii]).

For hospital-based IOPs, the reimbursed payments cover the provider's overhead costs, support staff, and the services of certified clinical social workers, occupational therapists, and alcohol and addiction counselors, whose "services are considered to be included in the . . . IOP rate" (TRICARE Reimbursement Manual 6010.61-M, Chapter 13, Section 2, 2018).[13] Unlike the Medicare system, which did away with distinctions between partial hospital and IOPs, TRICARE maintained a two-tiered system. One occurrence of the IOP code for either substance use disorder or psychiatric health treatment constitutes the lowest tier (TRICARE Reimbursement Manual 6010.61-M, Chapter 13, Section 2, 2018.).[14] The maximum reimbursement for an IOP is the PHP per diem (TRICARE Reimbursement Manual 6010.61-M Chapter 13, Section 2, 2018).

Reimbursement for freestanding IOPs is under the per diem payment system (32 CFR 199.2). The maximum allowable per diem rate is 75 percent of the rate for a full-day PHP, which are updated annually by the Medicare update factor used for the Inpatient Prospective Payment System for inpatient psychiatric facilities (32 CFR 199.14[a][2][ix][A][2]). The maximum per diem rate for a full-day PHP is 40 percent of the "average inpatient per diem amount per case established under the TRICARE mental health per diem reimbursement system during the fiscal year for both high and low volume psychiatric hospitals and units" (32 CFR 199.14[a][2][ix][A][2]). In sum, the

---

[13] The TRICARE manual emphasizes that hospitals do not bill the contractor for the professional services of the certified clinical social workers, occupational therapists and counselors, but rather that the "hospital's costs associated with [their] services shall continue to be billed to the contractor and paid through the per diem rate" (TRICARE Reimbursement Manual 6010.61-M, Chapter 13, Section 2, 2018).

[14] The Healthcare Common Procedure Coding System codes are S9480 and H0015 for intensive outpatient psychiatric services and alcohol and/or drug services, respectively.

freestanding IOP per diem rate is 75 percent of the PHP per diem rate, which is 40 percent of the average inpatient per diem rate.

The per diem is then adjusted according to the Medicare Inpatient Psychiatric Facility Prospective Payment System using patient and facility characteristics. One facility characteristic is geographic differences. For example, in fiscal year 2020, rural inpatient psychiatric facilities received a 17 percent wage adjustment. With respect to patient characteristics, adjustments may be made for age, specified comorbidities, length of stay, and the Medicare Severity Diagnosis Related Group (Medicare Learning Network, 2020, p. 4). Annual updates also occur: the Market Basket updates (i.e., to account for inflation in the cost of medical services) and Pricer updates (CMS, undated; Medicare Learning Network, 2020, p. 8).

IOPs must accept the per diem amount as payment in full for all IOP services. The CWC director of business operations said that TRICARE's reim-bursement rate for IOPs is fair and on par with other insurers.[15] This is con-sistent with recent analysis by TheraThink, an insurance billing firm, which reported that TRICARE reimbursement rates for different mental health care billing codes are average compared with private insurance compa-nies; the firm also reported that TRICARE is difficult to bill (TheraThink, undated).

The TRICARE Reimbursement Manual provides an exhaustive list of all services and supplies that are included in the per diem, regardless of whether they are billed separately. They are as follows (TRICARE Reim-bursement Manual 6010.61-M, Chapter 7, Section 2, 2017):

- Board. Includes use of the partial hospital facilities such as food service, supervised therapeutically constructed recreational and social activities, etc.
- Patient assessment. Includes the assessment of each individual accepted by the facility, and must, at a minimum, consist of a physical examination; psychiatric examination; psychological assessment; assessment of physiological, biological and cognitive processes; developmental assessment; family history and assessment; social history and assessment; educational or voca-

---

[15] Discussion with Jonathan Smith, April 7, 2021.

tional history and assessment; environmental assessment; and recreational/activities assessment.

- Psychological testing and assessment.
- Treatment services. All services including routine nursing services, group therapy, supplies, equipment and space necessary to fulfill the requirements of each patient's individualized diagnosis and treatment plan (with the exception of the psychotherapy . . .). All mental health services must be provided by an authorized individual professional provider of mental health services. [Exception: . . . IOPs that employ individuals with master's or doctoral level degrees in a mental health discipline who do not meet the licensure, certification and experience requirements for a qualified mental health provider but are actively working toward licensure or certification, may provide services within the all-inclusive per diem rate but the individual must work under the clinical supervision of a fully qualified mental health provider employed by the . . . IOP.]
- Ancillary therapies. Includes art, music, dance, occupational, and other such therapies.
- Overhead and any other services for which the customary practice among similar providers is included as part of the institutional charges.

Services that are *not* included in the IOP per diem rate may be billed separately include the following (TRICARE Reimbursement Manual 6010.61-M, Chapter 7, Section 2, 2017):

- Psychotherapy Sessions: Professional services provided by an authorized individual professional provider (who is not employed by or under contract with the . . . IOP) for purposes of providing clinical patient care to a patient in the . . . IOP may be cost-shared when billed by the individual professional provider. Any obligation of a professional provider to provide services through employment or contract in a facility or distinct program of a facility would preclude that professional provider from receiving separate TRICARE reimbursement on a fee-for-service basis to the extent that those services are covered by the employment or contract arrangement. Psychotherapy services provided outside of the employment/contract arrangement can be reimbursed separately from the PHPs or IOPs per diem.

- Primary/Attending Provider: When a patient is approved for admission to a[n] IOP, the primary or attending provider (if not contracted or employed by the partial program) may provide psychotherapy only when the care is part of the treatment environment which is the therapeutic partial program. That is why the patient is there—because that level of care and that program have been determined as medically necessary. The therapy must be adapted toward the events and interactions outlined in the treatment plan and be part of the overall partial treatment plan. Involvement as the primary or attending is allowed and covered only if he is part of the coherent and specific plan of treatment arranged in the partial setting. The treatment program must be under the general direction of the psychiatrist employed by the program to ensure medication and physical needs of the patients are met and the therapist must be part of the treatment team and treatment plan. An attending provider must come to the treatment plan meetings and his/her care must be coordinated with the treatment team and as part of the treatment plan. Care given independent of this is not covered.

- Non-Mental Health Related Medical Services: Those services not normally included in the evaluation and assessment of a partial hospitalization patient and not related to care in the . . . IOP. These medical services are those services medically necessary to treat a broken leg, appendicitis, heart attack, etc., which may necessitate emergency transport to a nearby hospital for medical attention. Ambulance services may be cost-shared when billed for by an authorized provider if determined medically necessary for emergency transport.

Payment is not due for leave days, days on which no treatment is provided, days the patient does not keep their appointment, or for days during which the services provided took less than three hours. With respect to billing, freestanding IOPs use the CMS 1450 UB-04 billing form and the CMS 1500 Claim Form for outpatient services (TRICARE Policy Manual, Chapter 11, Addendum G, 2017). There is no cost sharing for active-duty service members who obtain treatment at private-sector IOPs.

Accessing IOPs

Active-duty service members must be referred by their provider at the military installation to an IOP for treatment and, if the IOP is not local, travel and find lodging. We were told that TRICARE will not authorize payment for intensive treatment unless the requirements for necessity to receive a higher level of care are met prior to referral for care.[16]

Referral to an IOP

TRICARE policy requires a primary care manager referral for all IOP services. If the IOP is in the TRICARE network, a preauthorization from the network provider may be substituted (TRICARE Policy Manual, Chapter 7, Section 3.5). All of the program personnel with whom we spoke (detailed in Chapter Four and Appendixes A and B) addressed referrals only and not preauthorization. According to Kimberleigh Stickney, military and veteran coordinator and trauma therapist, the required referral process "can take a lot of time."

According to UCF Restores's Potts, active-duty service member referrals usually come from out of state. Sometimes, the referring provider will call the UCF Restores program to inquire whether a patient is a good fit for the IOP. The case coordinator then asks for the patient to contact UCF Restores for an eligibility screening and risk assessment, with the resulting information being given to the IOP directors. If confirmed to be a good fit for the program, UCF Restores will ask the service member to begin the process for obtaining TDY orders.

Potts noted that UCF Restores does not require active-duty service members to be on TDY, but it is up to the service member and the commanding officer to make the determination.[17]

An important note is that active-duty service members are often sent to IOPs as they go through the Integrated Disability Evaluation System process, pursuant to their eventual separation from the military.[18] Most of the

---

[16] Correspondence with Dr. Kate McGraw, September 29, 2021.

[17] Discussion with Monica Potts, April 13, 2021.

[18] See, for example, Preston, 2018, p. 111; also, see discussion with Kimberleigh Stickney, April 7, 2021.

individuals we spoke to noted that a significant proportion of patients are going through the disability evaluation process, referred to as the *medical board process*, or considering it. Kimberleigh Stickney, military and veteran coordinator and trauma therapist, mentioned that they see more active-duty patients who are going through the medical board process than are not. She said that the referral process does not change for patients who are, or eventually will be going through the disability evaluation process, "just the outcome is different."[19]

As Kerrie Earley said, an active-duty service member might be sent to a civilian IOP rather than be treated at an MTF if it is likely that the service member will be going through the medical board process to remain with the civilian provider afterward.[20] Air Force CMSgt (ret.) Andrew Laning, UHS divisional director of military programs, mentioned that recently about 50 percent of active-duty service members are eventually sent through the disability evaluation process, though the percentage used to be higher.[21] Chimnemerem Neal told us that of the 52 active-duty referrals they have received so far in 2021, 20 of them were going through or being considered for medical discharge.[22]

Traveling and Lodging at an IOP

Service members who travel on official orders to a medical facility for treatment within the local area may still be reimbursed for transportation, or the TDY mileage rate for travel with a private vehicle. If service members travel without official orders for said treatment, transportation is not reimbursable (DoD, 2022a).

Most service members who are outpatients away from their permanent duty station are on TDY, also known as temporary additional duty in the Navy and Marines (DoD, 2022c). Service members may also be sent to IOPs on other orders, although only with TDY orders, as explained below, are

---

[19] Discussion with Kimberleigh Stickney, April 7, 2021.

[20] Discussion with Kerrie Earley, April 14, 2021.

[21] Discussion with Air Force CMSgt (ret.) Andrew Laning II, April 22, 2021.

[22] Case study discussion with Chimnemerem Neal and Tracy Jones-Williams, April 27, 2021.

travel and housing reimbursed. Patients enrolled in IOPs are outpatients, and generally speaking do not require overnight accommodations. For private-sector programs, only room, and not board, is covered in the per diem rate (TRICARE Reimbursement Manual 6010.61-M, Chapter 7, Section 2, 2017). The DoD Financial Management Regulation outlines per diem policies for TDY both at and away from an installation as it pertains to dining and use of government quarters (DoD 7000.14-R, 2022).

Active-duty service members may be referred to IOPs that are outside the local area and require an overnight stay. A service member who is an outpatient away from the permanent duty station on TDY is eligible for a travel and transportation per diem. According to the Joint Travel Regulations, outpatient status means the patient does not have a bed assigned to them but is in a *non-leave status*. The per diem is authorized for when the service member "is in an outpatient status away from the PDS [permanent duty station] and for days of travel to, from, and between hospitals"(DoD, 2022c, p. 3D-1). The Joint Travel Regulation notes that an outpatient receives the "standard travel and transportation allowances," which includes lodging, meals and incidentals (DoD, 2022b; DoD, 2022c). For private-sector programs, we were told that getting TDY approval in a timely fashion can be difficult, not surprisingly, because it requires coordination between the military and civilian treatment facilities and the service member's command.[23]

Clinical Management

Topics unique to clinical management aspects of providing mental health and substance abuse treatment for an active-duty population require attention and nonmilitary providers should be aware of military-specific policies.

Confidentiality Policies

Active-duty service members are expected to be medically ready for duty (DoDI 6025.19, 2020). Various health conditions require medical attention, and service members may be placed on a temporary profile while receiving

---

[23] Discussion with Monica Potts, April 13, 2021.

treatment until the condition resolves (Department of the Army Regulation 40-502, 2019; Manual of the Medical Department, 2005; Department of the Air Force Manual 48-123, 2020). Commanding officers must track the fitness of their service members and they can access protected health information that would otherwise be private and protected in civilian settings.

The Military Command Exception to HIPAA, found in 45 CFR 164.512, provides that a *covered entity* may, but is not required to, disclose the personal health information of a service member for authorized activities to the appropriate military command authorities (45 CFR 164.512, 2016).[24] The authorized activities include determining fitness for duty, ability to perform a particular assignment, or to carry out any activity that is essential to the mission (DHA Privacy and Civil Liberties Office, 2022).

DoDI 6904.08 is essentially a carveout from the Military Command Exception. Whereas the Military Command Exception allows but does not require the sharing of personal health information with command, the DoDI prohibits providers from informing command when a service member obtains mental health or substance use education, with nine exceptions to that. It says, "providers shall notify the commander concerned" when service members' presentation includes: (1) harm to self, (2) harm to others, (3) harm to "specific military operational mission," (4) special personnel, (5) inpatient mental health or substance abuse treatment, (6) acute medical conditions interfering with duty, (7) formal inpatient or outpatient substance abuse treatment program participation, (8) command directed mental health evaluation, and (9) "other special circumstances." Health care providers who are employed as personal services contractors are subject to (1) the same credentialing review as military and civil service health care providers and (2) the same quality assurance, risk management, and clinical privileging standards (DoDI 6025.5, 1995).

DoDI 6025.18 details the implementation of HIPAA policies for DoD health programs. Across DoD policies related to sharing protected health information with DoD commanders, guidance to health providers is to share the minimum necessary information. DoD behavioral health care

---

[24] *Covered entity* is defined as a health plan or a health care provider that transmits any health information in electronic form in connection with a HIPAA standard transaction (45 CFR 164.512, 2016).

providers are made aware of and trained on how to implement DoD and service-level policies. We did not review training policies for private-sector providers; thus, we have not identified ways in which non-DoD providers receive guidance to implement DoD and service-level policies related to reporting requirements, exceptions to confidentiality, and the processes and procedures for engaging a service member's command.

Substance abuse is a health condition that is specifically reportable. When service members self-refer to treatment for substance abuse, policies are in place to prevent administrative consequences (i.e., disciplinary action). DoDI 1010.04, which was updated May 2020, "Establishes policies, assigns responsibilities, and prescribes procedures for problematic alcohol and drug use prevention, identification, diagnosis, and treatment for DoD military and civilian personnel." Department of the Army Regulation 600-85, updated in August 2020, describes the Army Substance Abuse Program and defines responsibilities, policies and procedures for identification and treatment, and legal and administrative procedures.

Given the TRICARE network accreditation and credentialing procedures required, private clinicians treating service members adhere to DoD healthcare delivery policies, but a complicating factor for training is that each service branch employs slightly different clinical policies for the management of substance abuse. For instance, SECNAVINST 5300.28F, provides guidance on impaired driving; AFI 44-121, updated November 2019, includes guidance on many relevant aspects of managing substance abuse, such as continuity of care for members of the Air Force who are enrolled in alcohol and drug abuse treatment programs, and procedures for maintaining medical records. Non-DoD clinicians need some level of familiarity with the military structure to understand the applicability of the policies depending on the service member in treatment. We did not review provider training material, which should be done to determine whether non-DoD providers are equipped with the requisite knowledge to adhere to DoD medical readiness policies.

Confidentiality in Practice

Laning emphasized the importance of communication between the private-sector IOP staff and the patient's command and military medical provider as a critical practice. The communications have two main goals. One goal is accountability and keeping the command informed of process-related information such as if the person arrived for the program; the second goal is to communicate information to medical staff. If command asks about medical information, the IOP staff refer them to the participant's medical provider to ensure HIPAA is followed. Also, in an effort to coordinate better with the military facility, attempts are made to use the same measurement (such as the PHQ-9 Depression Scale) at the start and end of the program and on a weekly basis, but it was noted that outcome measures may be different at different locations to tailor measures to their needs. Laning explained that when command calls, they do not typically need to know about the individual's life traumas; that information is given only to the referring medical personnel, and they instruct command to ask the medical personnel.

Laning reported that trusted relationships are constructed over time and recognizes that "we have to consider ourselves as an extension of who they [installation/base] are and that we have to work hand in hand with the base because they are responsible for that person [service member]." He clarified that the type of communication varies, stating that "command needs to know fitness for duty and the medical person [referring provider] wants to make sure we are meeting the medical necessities of the active-duty patients."

Laning further explained that their programs maintain clear communication with command about whether the service member patients are attending the program as planned. If a service member does not show up or misses appointments, the program will relay this information to command because they understand that the military is ultimately responsible for that member.

Laning also acknowledged the balance between protecting a service member's confidentiality while ensuring command can evaluate fitness for duty; under 10 U.S.C., command can technically request any information without the program violating HIPAA. However, Laning instructs his staff to only provide progress notes or information about the patient's trauma to the referring medical provider, who can then have a conversation with command about fitness for duty.[25]

According to Newins, because UCF Restores is a private-sector program that collects research data and does not receive any TRICARE funding, the program abides by HIPAA and does not release any information about active-duty patients unless the patient provides a release to do so. Newins acknowledged that she informs her active-duty patients that there may be very real consequences for not releasing any information if that is what the patient prefers. Moreover, UCF Restores does not confirm the presence of any of its active-duty patients unless the patient gives permission to reveal such a presence to command. If a member of the military contacts the program to inquire about a patient, the UCF Restores protocol is to invite the military personnel to contact the service member they are inquiring about and have them contact the Restores staff about disclosing any information.

According to Lisa Di Fiori, all patients at CWC are required to sign a release of information form, which allows the program to share information with the referring provider via weekly update reports.[26] Furthermore, the Florida Department of Children and Families requires CWC to send to certain assessments and treatment records to the other treating providers.[27]

The protocol for protecting patient confidentiality also remains if the service member patient discloses their substance use to a clinician. Newins noted that their program screens for substance use prior to entry and requires that substance use "be under control for two weeks" before the patient arrives to the program.[28] UCF Restores's Potts confirmed this policy but added that, if an active-duty patient revealed a safety issue around substance use (e.g., a pilot who drinks alcohol before going into the cockpit), the clinician would encourage the patient to discuss the behavior and help the patient find a way to speak to command about the issue.[29]

---

[25] Discussion with Air Force CMSgt (ret.) Andrew Laning II, March 22, 2021.

[26] Email from Lisa Di Fiori, August 5–6, 2021; discussion with Kimberleigh Stickney, April 7, 2021.

[27] Email from Lisa Di Fiori, August 5–6, 2021.

[28] Discussion with Amie Newins, April 6, 2021.

[29] Discussion with Monica Potts, April 13, 2021.

Walter Reed's Earley acknowledged that the systems in place to report sexual assault can be really complicated for her active-duty patients at her facility. She stressed the importance of the patient needing to understand the difference between a restricted and unrestricted report, how command handles those reports, and how to reintegrate back into service with people who may know something traumatic happened to them.[30]

Psychotherapeutics

Some service members receive psychotropic medication to treat their PTSD and/or depression. DoDI 6490.07 specifies medical conditions that would limit deployment for service members. In regard to medication for psychological conditions (such as PTSD or depression), the DoDI indicates medications can be used during a deployment if they will be consistently available in theater, do not require special handling, and do not cause problematic side effects (DoDI 6490.07, 2010).

Psychotherapeutics in Practice

We learned about how the four programs handle medication. CWC's Baker reported having a medical clinic with full medical services on site, with the exception of medical detox from substance dependence and labs with which to analyze urinalysis samples. Medical personnel consists of a medical director; an advanced registered nurse practitioner to manage such services as medication-assisted treatment for substance use disorders and to coordinate such adjunctive therapies as electroconvulsive therapy and transcranial magnetic stimulation; and a psychiatric physician's assistant to handle psychotropic medication management. Di Fiori reported that the Joint Commission standards for medical services and medication management help ensure that the highest levels of attention to issues of patient safety are in place.

The UCF Restores program had a psychiatrist on staff in the past, but the services were not used enough to make the position financially feasible in the long term. Staff observed that most patients arrive to the program with psychotropic medications already prescribed and noted that they col-

---

[30] Discussion with Kerrie Earley, April 14, 2021.

lect information about existing medication regimens during the screening process. Staff pay particularly close attention to anxiety symptoms and benzodiazepine prescriptions and may discuss with the prescribing provider about whether the patient may be able to forgo such medications while enrolled in the program.[31]

In the Evolution IOP at Landstuhl, staff reported that patients retain their existing psychiatrists. The program has a medication conciliation group that works to avoid inadvertent medication errors such as omissions, duplications, dosing errors, or drug interactions across transitions in care by comparing a patient's medication orders to all of the medications that the patient has been taking.

Medical Record Charting

TRICARE Policy Manual 6010.60-M emphasizes the importance of maintaining accurate patient records, and notes that in the mental health field, "the lack of pertinent information has often made it impossible to determine the patient's clinical condition, actual treatment rendered, the quality and effectiveness of the care provided, or the identity and qualifications of the staff providing treatment services." The TRICARE policy is that the medical record should contain an "adequate chronological report of the patient's course of care and should reflect any change in condition and the results of treatment." The record should include all significant information and be subject to utilization review and quality assurance. Providers must maintain contemporaneous clinical records of care (TRICARE Policy Manual 6010.60-M, Chapter 1, Section 5.1, 2020).

The minimum requirements for IOPs are set forth by the Joint Commission, CARF, COA or other accrediting organization approved by the DHA

---

[31] Benzodiazepines, for example, are typically recommended for short-term treatment of severe anxiety, panic, or insomnia. However, they are not recommended for the treatment of PTSD given the associations with worse overall symptom severity, aggression, depression, and substance use (Guina et al., 2015). Moreover, benzodiazepines are associated with worse psychotherapy outcomes (Guina et al., 2015), in part, because of the prevailing consensus among behavioral health providers that their effectiveness in providing short-term relief from distressing feelings are antithetical to one of the primary mechanisms of PTSD treatments (e.g., learning how to stop avoiding distressing situations, memories, and emotions).

director. Furthermore, the following documentation is required (TRICARE Policy Manual 6010.60-M, Chapter 1, Section 5.1, 2020):

- admission evaluation report, including baseline assessments using standardized measures for the diagnosis of PTSD, GAD, and Major Depressive Disorder (MDD) within 24 hours of admission
- completed history and physical examination report within 72 hours of admission
- registered nursing notes at the end of each shift
- daily physician notes.

The following standardized measures are also required at treatment baseline, at 60 to 120 day intervals, and at discharge, where relevant for the diagnosis:

- for PTSD, the PTSD Checklist (PCL)
- for GAD, the GAD-7
- for MDD, the Patient Health Questionnaire-8 (PHQ-8) (TRICARE Policy Manual 6010.60-M, Chapter 1, Section 5.1, 2020).

According to TRICARE, the four broad types of information that should be in the psychiatric record are

- administrative information for patient identification
- assessments obtained through examination, testing, and observation
- treatment planning
- documentation of care (TRICARE Policy Manual 6010.60-M, Chapter 1, Section 5.1, 2020).

The psychiatric record must also include the clinician's progress notes that relate to the goals and objectives outlined in the patient's treatment plan. The notes must contain information that enable verification that the services rendered were medically necessary and appropriate (TRICARE Policy Manual 6010.60-M, Chapter 1, Section 5.1, 2020).

Each service branch has policies on the types of medical records to be maintained, such as progress notes, treatment plans, and discharge summaries.[32] Not all of this guidance is publicly available, which is a complicating factor for private-sector medical personnel. Those providers are both unable to access and view the service member's electronic medical record, and they are unable to access some policies on documentation requirements.

Medical Record Charting in Practice

Earley indicated that referring MTF providers have access to group and individual therapy progress notes, individual treatment plans, and patient records in both the BHDP and AHLTA.

Potts at UCF Restores explained that the program uses an online records request system, but that records are only shared with the patient. If a referring provider would like to access a patient's records or set up a visit while the patient is in the IOP, the patient must provide authorization to do so.

Potts reported that she will typically have a discussion with the patient about the pros and cons of providing a release of records before a joint decision is made. For example, the patient might authorize a verbal release in which Potts can simply say that the patient is attending and completed the program while not disclosing details of the presenting problem (i.e., trauma type). Other times, the patient might authorize the release of the intake and discharge summaries following a discharge planning session once the patient has reached the end of the program. Potts emphasized that, in all instances, the patient must voluntarily ask for a release of records.[33]

Summary

We documented policies governing the approvals required to operate a DoD or private-sector mental health or substance abuse IOP. A participation agreement, facility or program accreditation, and jurisdictional licensing are part of a program's authorization. Program directors and administrators with whom we spoke indicated that these requirements are similar to those of other insurance panels. Although we did not review claims procedures, we noted some complaints about administrative challenges in navi-

---

[32] See, for example, AFI 44-102, 2012.

[33] Discussion with Monica Potts, April 13, 2021

gating claims submissions and, in particular, with receiving reimbursement from TRICARE. Credentialing of IOP providers is required by TRICARE, a process that involves a review of providers' education, training, liability coverage, professional license, work history, and other related information.

Credentialed military providers are expected to adhere to DoD policies regarding the delivery of health care for service members. This requirement is particularly noteworthy because providers are beholden to military regulations that (1) assume a level of knowledge and familiarity with the military and medical readiness and (2) specify unique reporting requirements when a service member's commander should be notified of the patient's health status. Military confidentiality standards differ from those afforded to civilians. We found that requirements for medical record documentation are typically specified by accreditation agencies. TRICARE requires mental health IOPs to administer and track standardized psychological assessment measures.

Our discussions with private-sector program directors and administrators suggest that the programs are able to navigate TRICARE requirements, receive referrals from military providers, and deliver treatment to active-duty service members. Nevertheless, our findings suggest that some policies and procedures governing the operation of and referral to IOPs could serve as barriers even as others help facilitate the private-sector program success, as described in Table 4.2. Policies that might hinder successful partnering with private-sector IOPs warrant further attention as DHA considers whether, how, and where to house IOPs.

TABLE 4.2
Policy Barriers and Facilitators for Private-Sector IOPs for PTSD

Policy Area	Reference	Barrier	Facilitator
Accreditation for DoD and private-sector facilities	DHA Procedures Manual 6025.13, Vol. 5; TRICARE Policy Manual, Chapter 11, Section 2.7		High standards lead to higher-quality patient care and safety protocols.
Payment and reimbursement	32 CFR 199.14; TRICARE Reimbursement Manual 6010.61-M, Chapter 13, Section 2	Claim rejections and slow payments	Reimbursement rate is fair.
Referrals	TRICARE Policy Manual 6010.61-M, Chapter 7, Section 3.5	Required referral process can be time-consuming	
Travel and lodging	Joint Travel Regulations, Chapter 3, Part D, Par. 0330	TDY orders can be time-consuming; TDY payments come from unit funds[a]	

[a] Discussion with Charles Engel, August 4, 2021.

CHAPTER FIVE

Knowledge Gaps and Additional Areas of Study

DoD is invested in maintaining the health and readiness of its fighting force, and sexual harassment and sexual assault in the military have significant personnel, personal, and financial consequences. Previously, RAND researchers reported that, in the 28 months following the 2014 RAND Military Workplace Study (Morral, Gore, and Schell, 2014), DoD lost 16,000 manpower hours as a result of military separation by those active-duty service members who were categorized as having been sexually harassed or sexually assaulted (Morral et al., 2021a). Providing effective treatment to these victims could help prevent such costly outcomes.

DoD is evaluating the effectiveness of five private-sector IOPs and two IOPs located within MTFs under the Sexual Trauma Intensive Outpatient Program TRICARE pilot study. The prevalence analysis, programmatic review, and policy review described in this report are intended to supplement DoD's efforts to assess the feasibility and advisability of using IOPs to treat PTSD, depression, substance misuse, and other psychological conditions resulting from sexual trauma.

In addition to the findings reported in the previous chapters, our reviews revealed many knowledge gaps surrounding the experiences, treatment needs, and effectiveness of different treatment components and models of care for active-duty victims of sexual harassment and sexual assault experiencing PTSD and related mental health problems. These knowledge gaps suggest additional areas of study that PHCoE and DHA will want to explore to further their understanding of this important area. Some of the important research questions that remain are as follows.

What are the treatment preferences of active-duty victims of sexual harassment and sexual assault with psychological health needs?

Our analysis highlights the need to collect data on the preferences of this population for seeking care in the private sector versus direct care at an MTF. Furthermore, it would be useful to understand why certain active-duty service members might prefer a private-sector IOP; understanding those reasons might help DoD improve care at MTFs. Treatment preferences might depend on patient characteristics and experiences. For instance, servicemen and women may have different treatment preferences, and service members who identify as lesbian, gay, or bisexual or who do not identify as heterosexual may have different treatment preferences than their heterosexual counterparts.

Are IOPs effective from a treatment standpoint? If so, what makes such programs effective? Are they more effective than outpatient treatment programs for active-duty service members who have experienced sexual harassment or sexual assault while serving in the military? Are they cost-effective compared with treatment as usual?

First, it will be important to understand whether the benefits of IOP care exceed the benefits of less costly outpatient care for the targeted patient population, which is very challenging to assess. One study comparing the effectiveness of three models of inpatient treatment for PTSD revealed a host of considerations. Fontana and Rosenheck, 1997, compared treatment delivered with veterans in specialized long-stay inpatient PTSD units, short-stay specialized evaluation and brief-treatment PTSD units, and general psychiatric units, and they found that all three produced similar symptom reductions at the initial follow-up. Pre-post studies of a cohort that is enrolled in care are likely to observe symptom reductions, particularly in the short term, because people tend to engage in treatment when their symptoms are high. As a result, time alone could account for these pre-post symptom reductions. Fontana and Rosenheck, 1997, found that veterans in the long-stay unit reported that symptoms and social functioning returned to levels at the time of admission, while those in the short-stay PTSD unit did not. Fontana and Rosenheck, 1997, also reported on patient satisfaction and program costs and concluded that because long-term inpatient stays are associated with higher costs, poorer long-term outcomes, and less patient satisfaction than short-term stay units, the VA should restructure its inpatient

PTSD treatment. Similar studies could be undertaken by DoD to evaluate the IOP model of care compared with outpatient PTSD treatment and non-specialized PTSD outpatient treatment; any evaluation of levels of care must account for symptom severity because those veterans with more-severe symptoms tend to be referred for a higher level of specialty care.

Our program discussions revealed a variety of program components and treatment approaches. The experts we spoke with and the literature we reviewed raise important hypotheses and areas of study such as whether attrition rates or key features of an IOP (e.g., group therapy) predict the IOP's effectiveness. These and other key ingredients and moderators of treatment outcomes must be understood. Specifically, the group makeup (i.e., mix of gender, rank, trauma-types, medical board status) may contribute to the effectiveness of an IOP. Whether integrative medicine approaches including yoga, art, and equine therapies contribute to outcomes is yet another needed area of study. A few clinicians thought that combat trauma and sexual trauma should be addressed in separate cohorts, even though psychotherapy groups are typically nontrauma focused.

There are trade-offs associated with rolling and cohort-based admissions. For example, a rolling admissions model will have less wait time for program entrance; cohorts require time to have a sufficient group size to begin the IOP. Cohort-based admissions may provide the potential for stronger group cohesion, and, in turn, healing. On the other hand, rolling admissions could offer more opportunity to open up and trust new people, and for more senior members of the group to help mentor newer ones.

More information about the reimbursement process, referral, medical record charting, sharing protected health information with relevant military personnel, managing substance abuse, military readiness, and handling service members who are pursuing a medical board are some of the topics that warrant further study, as they may moderate program effectiveness and affect decisions about IOP operation.

We identified pockets of research on IOPs for service members who have experienced sexual trauma. Recent and ongoing research initiatives within the National Center for PTSD and, more broadly, through external partnerships in collaboration with the VA and U.S. military (Hilton et al., 2019; Hoyt and Staley Shumaker, 2021; Ragsdale et al., 2020; Bryan et al., 2018; Zalta et al., 2018; Held et al., 2020, Lande et al., 2011) will help answer many of the questions we have highlighted in this report. We learned of sponsored research evaluating IOPs for service members with combat-related PTSD, and Beidel and Newins are studying the efficacy of their IOP for military members who have experienced sexual trauma. Research on IOP effectiveness will need to be synthesized to understand how it compares with outpatient treatment and whether there is sufficient evidence to recommend it as a first-line therapy.

Is DoD equipped to meet the psychological health need(s) of these service members through direct or private-sector care?

A starting point for assessing demand is to determine current utilization rates of DoD and private-sector IOPs. DHA should assess the ability of DoD to meet the demand for care from active-duty service members who have experienced sexual harassment or sexual assault. Part of this step may be examining potential barriers to DoD IOPs, such as staffing shortages or downsizing in direct care. DHA should also examine the availability of private-sector IOPs should DoD's capacity fall short.

The clinicians and clinical directors with whom we spoke frequently reported that group therapy is a necessary ingredient of the IOP that served to solidify progress made in individual psychotherapy sessions. This is an area of research to test this hypothesis. If that hypothesis is correct, it will be important to understand the overall demand for services at each installation to determine whether there is a sufficient patient population to fill a group. If the patient population is not sufficient to fill a group, private-sector and VA programs may offer something the MHS cannot—group members experiencing the mental health consequences of sexual trauma. It appears there is a gap in knowledge related to a comprehensive and up-to-date directory of available IOPs in the private sector that could treat sexual assault and sexual harassment trauma sequelae (American Psychological Association, undated). Another factor to consider is why active-duty service members should be referred to the private sector for care for reasons other than capacity.

We did not review VA programs but learned of many initiatives underway to study IOPs for veterans recovering from a military sexual trauma. If DoD is not equipped to meet the needs of these service members, it will be important to examine VA's efforts and whether service members are better served by VA IOPs or by private-sector IOPs. Finally, where to host an IOP— at an MTF, at a VA, or in the private sector with cohorts that stay together at a hotel (building group cohesion) or with service members going home to their families or barracks after the treatment day—is an open question.

Further Consideration for DHA

As a next step, DHA may consider establishing a research road map for how best to address these and other knowledge gaps about optimal treatment approaches for active-duty service members with problems stemming from a sexual assault that occurred while in the military. Some key topics to include, as discussed previously and summarized in Table 5.1, are treatment effectiveness, patient preferences, and MHS and TRICARE capacity.

Consideration of clinical management and care coordination policies and procedures is also an important next step, particularly if referrals are made to private-sector programs. In our policy review, we did not identify standardized guidance for referring clinicians. Additional research to assess the availability of clear policies and procedures for behavioral health providers is needed. It may be informative to interview behavioral health providers to understand their current practices and their perceptions of outstanding treatment needs of this patient population. The referral and care coordination from outpatient treatment to an IOP and potentially back to outpatient treatment is multifaceted. Figure 5.1 depicts key topics for consideration at each stage in the clinical management cycle.

Conclusions

We addressed disparate pieces of the larger question posed by Congress in the FY 2019 NDAA's Section 702 as defined by PHCoE. We documented practices of IOPs and the policies governing authorization to illustrate how those policies are implemented in practice, but we did not evaluate these policies or practices. Systematic evaluation of these topics is a necessary next step to understanding the appropriateness of using IOPs to treat service members' mental health consequences of experiencing sexual trauma in the military. The review described in this report highlights the promising outcomes of IOPs and suggests that DoD should continue to evaluate the use of these programs to treat service members experiencing the mental health consequences of sexual trauma.

TABLE 5.1

Topics for Future Research

Approach	Research Areas
Treatment effectiveness	
Program evaluation	• Assess multiple program components, such as program length, treatment approaches, group size, and location • Standardize clinical procedures to enhance evaluation
Comparative effectiveness trials	• Compare outpatient programs with intensive outpatient programs • Compare direct-care with private-sector or VA outpatient and IOP
Patient Preferences	
Interview and survey	• Assess preferences for types of therapy, length, and setting • Consider preferences in subpopulations (e.g., at-risk groups)
MHS and TRICARE capacity	
Cost benefit analysis	• Determine demand for services • Assess availability of services in MTFs and in the private sector • Assess cost implications of treatment delivered in MTFs, VA, and private sector • Consider transaction costs of partnering with non-DoD organizations
Clinical management	
Provider assessment	• Evaluate clinical coordination procedures (e.g., referral, medical charting, discharge plans)
Policy analysis	• Assess appropriateness of existing travel and lodging reimbursement procedures

FIGURE 5.1

Clinical Management Considerations

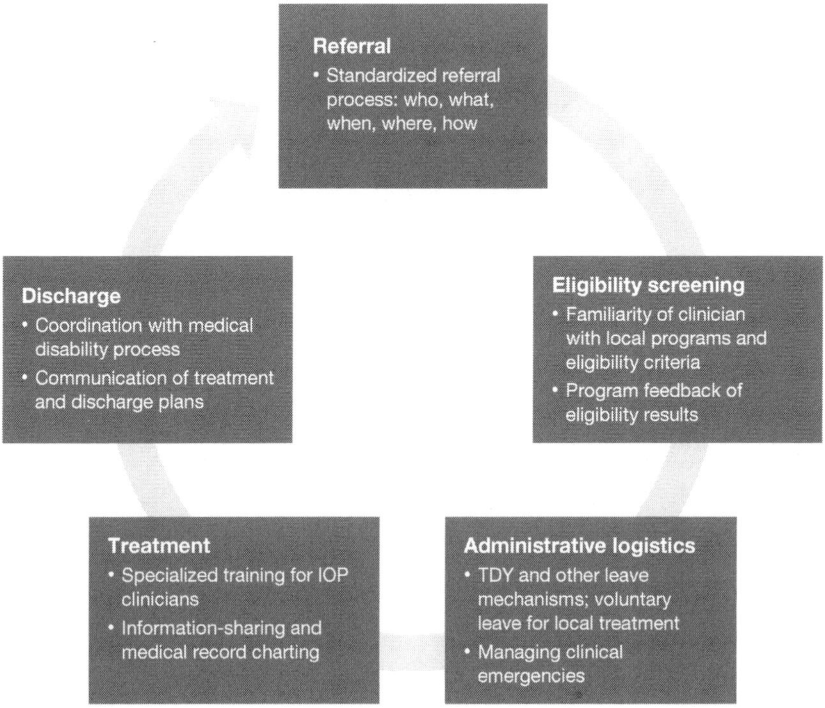

Referral
- Standardized referral process: who, what, when, where, how

Eligibility screening
- Familiarity of clinician with local programs and eligibility criteria
- Program feedback of eligibility results

Discharge
- Coordination with medical disability process
- Communication of treatment and discharge plans

Administrative logistics
- TDY and other leave mechanisms; voluntary leave for local treatment
- Managing clinical emergencies

Treatment
- Specialized training for IOP clinicians
- Information-sharing and medical record charting

Program Staff Discussion Guide

The discussion guide was divided into specific topic areas, and discussion topics were based on the individual's programmatic role (i.e., administrative versus clinical).

Introduction

This study is being conducted by the RAND Corporation, a nonprofit research institution located in Santa Monica, California. The study is being sponsored by the DoD's Psychological Health Center of Excellence (PHCoE), which is addressing the fiscal year (FY) 2019 National Defense Authorization Act (NDAA) authorization for the DOD to "carry out a pilot program to assess the feasibility and advisability of using intensive outpatient treatment programs" to address the psychological sequelae of sexual trauma for service members.

PHCoE commissioned RAND's National Defense Research Institute to support its efforts outside its pilot program, to conduct case studies comparing DoD, VA, and civilian PTSD intensive outpatient programs that provide services for survivors of military sexual assault within the military health and the civilian health systems. The purpose of the case studies is to understand different program components available to active-duty service members and veterans who have experienced sexual trauma and other trauma. This is not an evaluation of the work of these individuals or the program in any way.

A. Background
   1. What is your current title?
   2. How long have you worked in this position?
   3. (*MTF only*) What's your rank/grade? [Try to obtain status of civilian or military beforehand and which branch of military]
B. Program History
   4. What is/are the name(s) of the IOP program(s)?
   5. What year was the program established? How many years has the program treated patients?
   6. What motivated the development of the IOP?
   7. What populations do you serve? (gender, ages, race)
      a. (*MTF only*) Do you treat patients from other installations/services?
      b. NEW: Do you typically treat officers or enlisted more often? Or both?
      c. (*Civilian programs*) Do you treat patients that are not local?
   8. How many program tracks do you have and what are they? [*For civilian program only*] Are all of these available to active-duty service members/veterans?
   9. How was your program designed? What evidence-based practices were used to determine the treatment model?
      a (*MTF only*) How much of the program is based on guidance from the services/DHA versus developed independently?
   10. Do you have any material on the program design that you could provide to us? (e.g., theoretical framework, treatment decision tree).
C. Program Administration
   11. [*I am going to read through a list of approval processes. Can you please indicate if you went through these for your program, and what was involved?*] (Probe: time to complete paperwork, prepare for site visits, receive accreditation, costs associated with licenses, delays in program start etc.)
      a. Accreditation (Joint Commission, CARF, COA)
      b. State licensing
      c. Credentialing review (of providers' credentials)

        d.   Participation agreement

        e.   Other

12. What are the licensure and credentialing requirements for the different program providers? Must they be licensed in their state?

        a.   Do other program staff (administrators) have degree requirements?

13. How are staff trained to provide treatment specifically for this program?

   (If trained) Probe: certain curriculum, amount of time on training, trained before program start, during etc.

14. What is the registration or application process for individuals (patients) to participate in the IOP?

        a.   Are individuals referred to you?

        b.   Can individuals request enrollment without referral from a medical professional?

15. How common is it that the active-duty service members are going through the med-board process?

16. *(Civilian only)* What are the processes for reimbursement of costs for active-duty service members?

   Probe: calculation of the per diem, billing TRICARE etc.

17. *(MTF only)* Are there any costs to service-members/veterans for participating in the IOP? If so, who is billed?

18. How do you approach medical record access, review, and charting? To what extent are clinical notes shared with the referring provider?

19. What is the process for ensuring patient confidentiality? For active duty, how does this relate to command exception/fitness for duty and other reporting requirements (i.e., substance misuse) that presents during the program?

D.   Program Operations and Components

Operations

20. Describe admissions and IOP group sizes (rolling vs. cohort, minimum/maximum program size).

21. What is the program schedule?

        a.   How many days total is the program?

    b.   How many hours per day?

    c.   Is there any flexibility?

    d.   Can you walk us through a typical day for a participant?

22. Can you please describe what type of staff work in the IOP? Do you have an organizational chart you could share with us after this discussion?

23. What is the typical ratio of staff to participants?

24. *(Civilian only)* Do you combine active-duty service members with veterans or civilians in any of the treatment tracks?

25. To what extent can participants receive care virtually? Was this virtual option available before the pandemic? (virtual care options might include providing treatment via videoconference or telephone or working with patients to use mobile apps to treat or manage symptoms)

    a.   *(if yes)* What administrative practices are in place to help ensure access to care for those who do not have appropriate technology or internet?

26. Is housing and or/meals provided for participants? If so, please describe.

27. *(MTF only, if treats members from other installations)*: How does reimbursement for lodging for members from other installations work?

28. *(Civilian only)* Is transportation provided to individuals to attend the program, and if so, what type and how many people use the service?

29. If transportation isn't provided, is there reimbursement for the cost of travel? How does the process work?

30. Do you partner with other service providers to operate the IOP(s)? If so, with whom?

Components

31. What does patient intake consist of?

32. Do you provide individual therapy? If so, for how long and how frequently? (times per week)

33. [*For providers (therapists and/or prescribers) who deliver care for PTSD/trauma-related conditions*] What treatment approaches do you use to treat patients with PTSD and other trauma-related

conditions? Please describe your primary treatment approach and if it differs depending on the type of trauma (combat, sexual, accident, etc.).

    a.   Therapy approaches (e.g., trauma-focused cognitive behavioral therapy, such as cognitive processing therapy [CPT], prolonged exposure [PE], stress inoculation training, eye movement desensitization and reprocessing [EMDR], trauma- management therapy [TMT])

    b.   Medications prescribed (e.g., selective serotonin reuptake inhibitors [SSRIs]/serotonin-norepinephrine reuptake inhibitors [SNRIs])

34. Do you provide group therapy? If so, for how long and how frequently? (Times per week?)

    a.   What is the focus of each group therapy session? Who are the members of each group? Do you combine officers and enlisted in the same sessions?

    b.   Assess delivery of treatment (e.g., homework assigned, number of sessions of group versus individual therapy, structure of treatment, frequency and type of symptoms assessment during course of treatment)

35. What types of materials are provided to patients? (e.g., handouts, skill-building workbooks, required versus recommended reading materials).

    a.   How often are such materials provided to patients?

36. Do participants "graduate" from the IOP?

37. Is there any type of after-care that is offered? Booster session?

38. Are there treatment plans that are sent to some outpatient provider or case manager?

39. How do you handle referral to outpatient care for active-duty service members? If indicated, how would you "step-up" care to place an active-duty service member in residential (i.e., inpatient) care?

40. Does the program use nonmedical or integrative medicine approaches (i.e., yoga, art, meditation acupuncture)?

E.   Treatment Data

[I'd like to move to a few questions that address any data you may collect on program participants.]

41. Overall, what has been the impact of [program name]?
    a.   What differences in health have you noticed in the participants you serve as a result?
    b.   What factors have been key to achieving this impact?
    c.   What factors have impeded your progress?
42. What types of data do you collect on the program?
    Probe: program completion rate, program dropout rate, changes in behavioral health outcomes (e.g., reduction in substance use, reductions in suicidal ideation, etc.)
43. How many years of data do you have on the IOP?
44. What do you do with the data you collect?
    Probe: Used to change program design, refer participants to other medical professionals etc.?
45. How do patient characteristics affect care delivery, if at all? For example, active-duty service members who are going through a medical board. Or for those with physical injuries/amputees (do they get physical therapy, too)?

F.   Wrap-up

46. Is there anyone else you think we should speak to about the items we discussed today?
47. Is there anything else I didn't ask about that you think would be helpful for us to know about the IOP discussed today?

Methods for Program Identification and Selection

We held a total of 18 discussions with staff at medical centers, hospitals, and clinics. Discussions were held with 12 of those individuals at four IOPs, two in the private sector, and two on DoD installations, which we describe in detail in Chapter Three. Discussions focused on understanding the program processes and components and any particular barriers and facilitators to active component service members receiving treatment. In this appendix, we describe how we selected the four programs used as case studies in our analysis.

Program Identification

We used a convenience sampling approach and prespecified inclusion criteria to identify at least one DoD and one private-sector PTSD IOP program that provide treatment for active-duty service members who experienced sexual trauma in the military. We conducted open-source internet-based searches for programs and reviewed a limited number of known programs evaluated as part of a related systematic literature review conducted by RAND researchers, because there is currently no central database listing available IOPs serving this unique population.

The TRICARE website indicates that IOPs are available and how individuals may qualify. However, a list of IOPs was not available rather, and individuals are referred to contact a regional contractor regarding authorization (TRICARE, undated-a). Similarly, the Health Net and Humana websites for TRICARE did not provide further information on available IOPs outside those included in the TRICARE pilot study (Health Net Federal Services, undated; Humana Military, undated-a). Although there is a DoD Safe Helpline website that provides information on resources for individuals affected by sexual assault, no information on IOPs is readily available (DoD Safe Helpline, undated).

Using terms such as "IOP" or "intensive outpatient program" in basic internet searches, we were able to identify programs that we believe may be helpful to others also looking for these programs. Internet searches through online databases, including *Psychology Today* filtered searches for providers by location, treatment type, and program type, including IOPs (Psychology Today, undated). In many cases individual outreach to organizations was needed to understand whether program characteristics met our program inclusion criteria.

We also met with senior officials within DHA and TRICARE. They shared a list of TRICARE West IOPs, including 53 programs, ten that offered a treatment track focused on PTSD, seven of those ten also offered a specific track to treat trauma due to sexual assault that occurred in the military. They shared a list of 152 TRICARE East programs identified using available claims data from 2018 to 2021. Among them, five programs were flagged as treating either sexual trauma that occurred in the military, or PTSD, or both.

Program Selection

We selected programs that treat a larger number of patients, had a greater time in existence, and may have had a higher reputation with military mental health providers, for the purposes of including a program that used evidence-based treatments and that may have data on relevant health outcomes. We searched for programs that would allow them to compare services for sexual assault-related PTSD relative to other PTSD at a DoD IOP and a private-sector IOP. Attempts were also made to identify IOPs located in known areas of need identified by TRICARE points of contact, specifically in the areas surrounding Fayetteville, North Carolina; San Antonio, Texas; and the Pacific Northwest around Joint Base Lewis-McCord, and considerations were made to reach out to private-sector IOPs located within a reasonable distance from military installations. Using these strategies, four programs were selected for inclusion representing examples of programs available to service members and veterans that are well-publicized or well-known programs in the scientific and clinical communities.

Outreach included RAND team members either emailing or calling program points of contact. RAND contacted 15 organizations with IOP programs, 11 of which were operating in the private sector, two programs within the VA, and two programs within DoD. One organization did not respond to our request, and three expressed initial interest but did not follow up with our attempted communications. Five provided information that determined they did not treat service members or did not treat the traumas related to sexual harassment or sexual assault. Several of these discussions revealed additional insights that may be of interest to DHA program administrators or network administrators.

We found that the UHS health system offers Patriot Support Programs, which include TRICARE-certified facilities that are seen as crucial to providing quality care because the certification ensures certain standards (UHS, Patriot Support Programs, undated-a; UHS, Patriot Support Programs, undated-b).[1] The Patriot Support Programs include IOPs for active-duty service members, one of which is in the Sexual Trauma Intensive Outpatient Program TRICARE Pilot in Salt Lake City, Utah. Laning, the UHS divisional director of military programs, shared that its 27 IOPs have different components and approaches. Referrals into any of the system's Patriot Support Programs are based on a program's proximity to a base or installation. For example, the Valley Hospital in Arizona is near Luke Air Force Base, and Poplar Springs Hospital is near Fort Lee in Petersburg, Virginia. Laning indicated that, although the IOPs may be addressing sexual trauma, individuals are enrolled based on such conditions as drug abuse or personality disorders. He said that a substantial portion of service members who are referred to the Patriot Support Programs are pursuing a medical board.[2] He also shared that for participants in IOPs, lodging can be a challenge,

---

[1] See also discussion with Air Force CMSgt (ret.) Andrew Laning II, April 22, 2021.

[2] Discussion with Air Force CMSgt (ret.) Andrew Laning II, April 22, 2021.

but that they try to house individuals on nearby military installations when possible because most of the IOPs do not have housing facilities.

We spoke to staff at Emerald Coast IOP, one of Patriot Support's earliest programs. Emerald Coast prides itself on its close relationships with the nearby military installations and explained that the programs cater to the mental health treatment needs of the military.[3] Emerald Coast includes three outpatient centers, each serving slightly different populations. The Fort Walton Beach location treats mostly active-duty service members with military trauma. Its IOP is a four- to six-week program. Blue Springs offers a military trauma IOP and a sexual trauma pilot program for active-duty service members and veterans. The Panama City location also has a military trauma track for active-duty service members and veterans.[4] The IOPs at Emerald Coast tend to receive active-duty service members from an inpatient facility, where they have been for two to four weeks, although they may also be referred directly to the IOP.

We learned the sexual trauma track at Blue Springs is for women only. They would place servicemen with sexual trauma into the combat trauma program. Patients at the IOPs are all admitted on a rolling basis, and the foundation of the program is three to six hours of group therapy per day, plus one hour of individual therapy and 30 to 60 minutes with a psychiatrist to discuss medication per week. In group therapy, treatments include CBT, DBT, individual therapy, and EMDR.[5]

The programs we ultimately selected as case illustrations represented a variety of programmatic examples. The four resulting programs that we engaged to help us understand TRICARE and private-sector IOP policies and practices were

- the U.S. Army's Evolution Trauma IOP located within the Landstuhl Regional Medical Center in Germany (Landstuhl Regional Medical Center, undated)

---

[3] Discussion with Robert Reuille, Craig Segrest, Jessica Kemp, and Jennifer Humphrey, April 2, 2021.

[4] Discussion with Robert Reuille, March 24, 2021.

[5] Appendix C contains a brief summary of these and other psychotherapy approaches.

- an IOP within the Psychiatry Continuity Service at the Walter Reed National Military Medical Center (Walter Reed National Medical Center, undated)
- the UCF Restores IOP located at the University of Central Florida (CWC, 2020)
- CWC's IOP located in Lantana, Florida (CWC, 2020).

We detail our discussions with 12 individuals implementing IOPs—ranging from operational and clinical directors and administrative staff and clinicians as outlined in Table B.1. We also spoke with five other individuals working for IOPs, which we describe generally.[6] In total, we spoke to 18 individuals in our data collection process.

TABLE B.1
Types of Individuals Interviewed

	Private Sector		DoD	
	CWC	UCF Restores	Evolution Trauma IOP	Walter Reed IOP
Director/CEO		1		
Clinical director	1	1		1
Clinician	1	1	2	1
Business operations	1	1		
Director of operations	1			
Military liaison	1			

NOTE: The total number in this table is higher than the total number of interviews because some individuals performed dual roles.

---

[6] We are unable to share the information provided by one individual working in an IOP, which was in a pilot stage and not yet at a phase where information from the program could be summarized.

Treatment Approaches for Posttraumatic Stress Disorder

Clinical practice guidelines prescribe evidence-based practices to treat specific conditions. Table C.1 describes specific therapeutic approaches based on PTSD treatment guidelines. It includes treatments specified by the program clinicians we interviewed. This is not an exhaustive list of all therapeutic approaches for PTSD.

TABLE C.1

Mental Health Treatment Approaches for Posttraumatic Stress Disorder and Related Conditions

Treatment Type	Description
General trauma-focused psychotherapy	Any therapy that uses cognitive, emotional, or behavioral techniques to facilitate processing a traumatic experience and in which the trauma focus is a central component of the therapeutic process (Schnurr, 2017). Treatment often involves eight to 16 sessions with varying combinations of the following core techniques: exposure to traumatic images or memories through narrative or imaginal exposure; exposure to avoided or triggering cues in vivo or through visualization; and cognitive restructuring techniques focused on enhancing meaning and shifting problematic appraisals stemming from the traumatic experience(s) (VA and DoD, 2017).
Accelerated resolution therapy	Emerging trauma-focused therapy that uses techniques, such as rapid eye movement, desensitization through imaginal exposure, and memory reconsolidation through imagery rescripting, to treat the effects of trauma (Kip and Diamond, 2018).

Table C.1—Continued

Treatment Type	Description
Brief eclectic psychotherapy	Has a strong psychodynamic perspective but also incorporates imaginal exposure, written narrative processes, cognitive restructuring through attention to meaning and integration of the experience, relaxation techniques, and a metaphorical ritual closing to leave the traumatic event in the past and foster a sense of control (VA and DoD, 2017).
CBT	Combines behavioral and cognitive interventions that aim to decrease maladaptive behaviors and increase adaptive ones, and modify maladaptive thoughts, self-statements, or beliefs (Craske, 2017).
CPT	Emphasizes cognitive restructuring through Socratic dialogue to examine problematic beliefs, emotions, and negative appraisals stemming from the event, such as self-blame or mistrust (VA and DoD, 2017).
DBT	A cognitive-behavioral approach that helps teach people how to live in the moment, develop healthy ways to cope with (dis)stress, regulate their emotions, and improve their relationships with others (Linehan Institute Behavioral Tech, undated). Originally intended to treat borderline personality disorder but has been adapted to treat other behavioral health conditions, including PTSD (Steil et al., 2018).
EMDR	Incorporates imaginal exposure through narration and visualization to process the worst image, emotion, and negative cognition associated with the traumatic event, along with a healthier cognitive reappraisal, with bilateral eye movements or other form of bilateral stimulation intended to create a dual awareness environment to facilitate processing and relaxation (VA and DoD, 2017).
Imaginal exposure	A common element of exposure-based treatments involving repeated and prolonged engagement, revisiting, and processing of the trauma memory. Occurs in session with the patient describing the traumatic event in the present tense, including as much detail about events, surroundings, sensations, thoughts, and feelings as he or she can remember with guidance from the therapist (Foa, Hembree, and Rothbaum, 2007).
Interpersonal psychotherapy	A nontrauma-focused psychotherapy that focuses on the effect that trauma has had on an individual's interpersonal relationships (VA and DoD, 2017).

Table C.1—Continued

Treatment Type	Description
In vivo exposure	A common element of exposure-based treatments involving systematic engagement and interaction with objectively safe trauma reminders in the environment. Is often done outside of session, working up a hierarchy of perceived difficulty and distress (Foa, Hembree, and Rothbaum, 2007).
Pharmacotherapy	Selective serotonin reuptake inhibitors (SSRI) (sertraline, paroxetine, fluoxetine) or serotonin-norepinephrine reuptake inhibitor (SNRI) (venlafaxine) as monotherapy for PTSD for patients diagnosed with PTSD who choose not to engage in or are unable to access trauma-focused psychotherapy (VA and DoD, 2017).
Narrative exposure therapy	Relies on imaginal exposure through a structured oral life-narrative process that helps patients integrate and find meaning in multiple traumatic experiences across their lifespan (VA and DoD, 2017).
Present-centered therapy	A nontrauma-focused psychotherapy that focuses on current problems in a patient's life that are related to PTSD (VA and DoD, 2017).
Prolonged exposure	Emphasizes imaginal exposure through repeatedly recounting the traumatic narrative out loud (often in present tense, eyes closed, reinforced by being asked to listen to an audio recording of the narrative process between treatment sessions). This is combined with in vivo exposure, and emotional processing of the narrative experience (VA and DoD, 2017).
Reconsolidation of traumatic memories	A brief, trauma-focused CBT derived from neuro-linguistic programming techniques used for PTSD characterized primarily by intrusive symptoms. The trauma memory is presented through three levels of dissociation, and perceptual modifications are applied to ensure or reinforce the memory's loss of immediacy; The process is immediately interrupted when the patient expresses discomfort, whether verbally or nonverbally (Gray, Budden-Potts, and Bourke, 2019).
Stress inoculation training	A nontrauma-focused form of cognitive restructuring targeting individual thinking patterns that lead to stress responses in everyday life (VA and DoD, 2017).

Table C.1—Continued

Treatment Type	Description
Trauma management therapy	Emerging behavioral trauma-focused therapy designed to specifically address the complex nature of PTSD through two broad treatment components: intensive individual exposure therapy, addressing the unique characteristics of each individual's traumatic event, and social and emotional rehabilitation, which uses a skills training approach and is delivered in a group format (Beidel, Frueh, et al., 2017).
Written exposure therapy	Brief trauma-focused intervention in which individuals are asked to write about their traumatic experiences following scripted instruction (Sloan et al., 2018)

Psychological Assessments Administered by the Intensive Outpatient Programs

In Table D.1, we provide brief descriptions of the psychological assessment interviews and questionnaires that were mentioned during our program discussions. A description of the psychometric properties of these instruments is beyond the scope of this project. Each program relied on different measures to assess patient health status and track outcomes. This is not an exhaustive list of psychological assessments that may be administered by IOPs.

TABLE D.1

Measures to Assess Patient Health Status and Track Outcomes

Measurement	Description
ADIS-5	A semistructured clinical interview designed to diagnose anxiety and mood disorders and several related disorders and to facilitate differential diagnosis among disorders using the Diagnostic and Statistical Manual of Mental Disorders, Fifth Edition (DSM-5) (Brown, Bourgeois, and Rutter, 2017).
AUDIT	A ten-item screening questionnaire developed by the World Health Organization to identify persons whose alcohol consumption has become hazardous or harmful to their health (Babor et al., 1992).
BAM-R	A 17-item, multidimensional, progress-monitoring instrument that assesses risk factors for substance use, protective factors that support sobriety, and drug and alcohol use (Hallinan et al., 2021).

Table D.1—Continued

Measurement	Description
CAPS-5	A 30-item structured interview that can be used to make current (past month) diagnosis of PTSD, make lifetime diagnosis of PTSD, and assess PTSD symptoms over the past week. In addition to assessing the 20 DSM-5 PTSD symptoms, questions target the onset and duration of symptoms, subjective distress, effect of symptoms on social and occupational functioning, improvement in symptoms since a previous CAPS administration, overall response validity, overall PTSD severity, and specifications for the dissociative subtype (depersonalization and derealization) (Weathers, Blake, et al., 2013a).
C-SSRS	A questionnaire designed to quantify the severity of suicidal ideation and behavior (Posner et al., 2011).
CUDIT-R	An eight-item cannabis screening tool used to capture important features of consumption patterns, cannabis problems (abuse), dependence symptoms, and psychological features (Adamson et al., 2010).
DAR-5	A five-item measure that assesses anger frequency, intensity, duration, aggression and effect on a person's social functioning over the preceding four-week period (Forbes et al., 2004; Forbes et al., 2014).
DAST-10	A ten-item measure that yields a quantitative index of the degree of consequences related to drug abuse (Skinner, 1982; Yudko, Lozhkina, and Fouts, 2007).
GAD-7	A seven-item self-report screening tool and symptom severity measure anxiety (Spitzer et al., 2006).
LEC-5	A self-report measure designed to screen for potentially traumatic events in a respondent's lifetime. Assesses exposure to 16 events known to potentially result in PTSD or distress and includes one additional item assessing any other extraordinarily stressful event not captured in the first 16 items (Weathers, Blake, et al., 2013b).
PHQ-9	A nine-item multipurpose instrument for screening, diagnosing, monitoring and measuring the severity of depression (Kroenke et al., 2010).
PCL-5	A 20-item self-report measure that assesses the 20 DSM-5 symptoms of PTSD. Used for a variety of purposes, including monitoring symptom change during and after treatment, screening individuals for PTSD, and making a provisional PTSD diagnosis (Weathers, Litz, et al., 2013).

Abbreviations

ADIS-5	Anxiety and Related Disorders Interview Schedule for DSM-5
AHLTA	Armed Forces Health Longitudinal Technology Application
AUDIT	Alcohol Use Disorders Identification Test
BAM-R	Brief Addiction Monitor-Revised
BHDP	Behavioral Health Data Portal
CAPS-5	Clinician-Administered PTSD Scale for DSM-5
CARF	Commission on Accreditation of Rehabilitation Facilities
CBT	cognitive behavioral therapy
CFR	Code of Federal Regulations
CMS	Centers for Medicare Services
COA	Council on Accreditation
CPT	cognitive processing therapy
C-SSRS	Columbia-Suicide Severity Rating Scale
CUDIT-R	Cannabis Use Disorders Identification Test-Revised
CWC	Comprehensive Wellness Center
DAR-5	Dimension of Anger-5
DAST-10	Drug Abuse Screening Test-10
DBT	dialectical behavior therapy
DHA	Defense Health Agency
DoD	U.S. Department of Defense
DSM	*Diagnostic and Statistical Manual of Mental Disorders*
EMDR	Eye Movement Desensitization and Reprocessing
FY	fiscal year
GAD-7	Generalized Anxiety Disorder-7

IOP	intensive outpatient program
LEC-5	Life Events Checklist for DSM-5
MDD	major depressive disorder
MHS	military health services
MTF	military treatment facility
NDAA	National Defense Authorization Act
PCL-5	PTSD Checklist for DSM-5
PHCoE	Psychological Health Center of Excellence
PE	prolonged exposure
PHP	partial-hospitalization program
PHQ	Patient Health Questionnaire
PTSD	posttraumatic stress disorder
SECNAVINST	Secretary of the Navy Instruction
SNRI	serotonin-norepinephrine reuptake inhibitor
SSRI	selective serotonin reuptake inhibitor
TDY	temporary duty
TMT	trauma-management therapy
VA	U.S. Department of Veterans Affairs
VHA	Veterans Health Administration
UCMJ	Uniform Code of Military Justice
UHS	Universal Health Services

References

32 CFR 199—*See* Code of Federal Regulations, Title 32, National Defense, Subtitle A. Department of Defense, Chapter I. Office of the Secretary of Defense, Subchapter M. Miscellaneous, Part 199. Civilian Health and Medical Program of the Uniformed Services (CHAMPUS).

32 CFR 199.2—*See* Code of Federal Regulations, Title 32, National Defense, Part 199, Section 2, Definitions.

32 CFR 199.6—*See* Code of Federal Regulations, Title 32, National Defense, Part 199, Section 6.

32 CFR 199.14—*See* Code of Federal Regulations, Title 32, National Defense, Part 199 Section 14.

38 U.S.C., § 1720D—*See* U.S. Code, Title 38, Veterans' Benefits, Chapter 17, Section 1720D, Counseling and Treatment for Sexual Trauma.

45 CFR 164.512—*See* Code of Federal Regulations, Title 45, Public Welfare, Subtitle A. Department of Health and Human Services, Subchapter C. Administrative Data Standards and Related Requirements, Part 164. Security and Privacy, Subpart E. Privacy of Individually Identifiable Health Information, Section 164.512. Uses and Disclosures for Which an Authorization or Opportunity to Agree or Object Is Not Required.

Adamson, S. J., F. J. Kay-Lambkin, A. L. Baker, T. J. Lewin, L. Thornton, B. J. Kelly, and J. D. Sellman, "An Improved Brief Measure of Cannabis Misuse: The Cannabis Use Disorders Identification Test–Revised (CUDIT-R)," *Drug and Alcohol Dependence*, Vol. 110, 2010, pp. 137–143.

American Psychological Association, "Sequela," *APA Dictionary of Psychology*, undated. As of April 8, 2021:
https://dictionary.apa.org/sequela

Atwoli, L., D. J. Stein, K. C. Koenen, and K. A. McLaughlin, "Epidemiology of Posttraumatic Stress Disorder: Prevalence, Correlates and Consequences," *Current Opinion in Psychiatry*, Vol. 28, No. 4, July 2015.

Babor, T. F., J. R. de la Fuente, J. Saunders, and M. Grant, *AUDIT: The Alcohol Use Disorders Identification Test. Guidelines for Use in Primary Health Care*, Geneva, Switzerland: World Health Organization, 1992.

Beidel, D. C., J. W. Stout, S.M. Neer, B. C. Frueh, and C. Lejuez, "An Intensive Outpatient Treatment Program for Combat-Related PTSD: Trauma Management Therapy," *Bull Menninger Clinic*, Vol. 81, No. 2, June 2017, pp. 107–122.

Beidel, D. C., B. C. Frueh, S. M. Neer, and C. W. Lejuez, "The Efficacy of Trauma Management Therapy: A Controlled Pilot Investigation of a Three-Week Intensive Outpatient Program for Combat-Related PTSD," *Journal of Anxiety Disorders*, Vol. 50, August 2017, pp. 23–32.

Breslin, R. A., L. Davis, K. Hylton, A. Hill, W. Klauberg, M. Petusky, and A. Klahr, *2018 Workplace and Gender Relations Survey of Active Duty Members: Overview Report*, Alexandria, Va.: U.S. Department of Defense, Office of People Analytics, OPA Report No. 2019-027, May 2019.

Brown, T. A., M. L. Bourgeois, and L. A. Rutter, "Anxiety and Related Disorders Interview Schedule for DSM-5," in Amy Wenzel, ed., *The Sage Encyclopedia of Abnormal and Clinical Psychology*, Thousand Oaks, Calif.: SAGE Publications, Inc., April 2017, pp. 210–211.

Bryan, Craig J., Feea R. Leifker, David C. Rozek, AnnaBelle O. Bryan, Mira L. Reynolds, D. Nicolas Oakey, and Erika Roberge, "Examining the Effectiveness of an Intensive, 2-Week Treatment Program for Military Personnel and Veterans with PTSD: Results of a Pilot, Open-Label, Prospective Cohort Trial," *Journal of Clinical Psychology*, Vol. 74, No. 12, December 1, 2018, pp. 2070–2081.

BUMED—*See* Bureau of Medicine and Surgery.

Bureau of Medicine and Surgery Instruction 6000.2F, *Accreditation of Fixed Medical Treatment Facilities*, Washington, D.C.: Department of the Navy, October 10, 2017.

Burton, Mark, Kathryn Black, Jessica Maples-Keller, Sheila Rauch, and Barbara Rothbaum, *Maintenance of Gains Following an Intensive Outpatient Program for PTSD*, Atlanta, Ga.: Thirty-Fifth Annual Convention of the International Society for Traumatic Stress Studies, November 15, 2019.

Campbell, R., E. Dworkin, and G. Cabral, "An Ecological Model of the Impact of Sexual Assault on Women's Mental Health," *Trauma Violence Abuse*, Vol. 10, No. 3, July 2009, pp. 225–246.

CARF—*See* Commission on Accreditation of Rehabilitation Facilities.

Centers for Medicare and Medicaid Services, "Market Basket Definitions and General Information," fact sheet, undated. As of May 25, 2021: https://www.cms.gov/Research-Statistics-Data-and-Systems/Statistics-Trends-and-Reports/MedicareProgramRatesStats/Downloads/info.pdf

CFR—*See* Code of Federal Regulations.

Chivers-Wilson, K. A., "Sexual Assault and Posttraumatic Stress Disorder: A Review of the Biological, Psychological and Sociological Factors and Treatments," *McGill Journal of Medicine*, Vol. 9, No. 2, July 2006, pp. 111–118.

CMS—*See* Centers for Medicare and Medicaid Services.

COA—*See* Council of Accreditation.

Code of Federal Regulations, Title 32, National Defense, Subtitle A. Department of Defense, Chapter I. Office of the Secretary of Defense, Subchapter M. Miscellaneous, Part 199. Civilian Health and Medical Program of the Uniformed Services (CHAMPUS), July 1, 1986.

Code of Federal Regulations, Title 32, National Defense, Subtitle A. Department of Defense, Chapter I. Office of the Secretary of Defense, Subchapter M. Miscellaneous, Part 199. Civilian Health and Medical Program of the Uniformed Services (CHAMPUS), Section 2, Definitions, July 1, 1986, last updated July 1, 2011.

Code of Federal Regulations, Title 32, National Defense, Subtitle A. Department of Defense, Chapter I. Office of the Secretary of Defense, Subchapter M. Miscellaneous, Part 199. Civilian Health and Medical Program of the Uniformed Services (CHAMPUS), Section 6, TRICARE–Authorized Providers, July 1, 1986, last updated July 1, 2021.

Code of Federal Regulations, Title 32, National Defense, Subtitle A. Department of Defense, Chapter I. Office of the Secretary of Defense, Subchapter M. Miscellaneous, Part 199. Civilian Health and Medical Program of the Uniformed Services (CHAMPUS), Section 14, Provider Reimbursement Methods, April 10, 1990, last updated July 1, 2021.

Code of Federal Regulations, Title 45, Public Welfare, Subtitle A. Department of Health and Human Services, Subchapter C. Administrative Data Standards and Related Requirements, Part 164. Security and Privacy, Subpart E. Privacy of Individually Identifiable Health Information, Section 164.512. Uses and Disclosures for Which an Authorization or Opportunity to Agree or Object Is Not Required, last updated January 6, 2016.

Commission on Accreditation of Rehabilitation Facilities, homepage, undated-a. As of May 26, 2021: http://www.carf.org/home

Commission on Accreditation of Rehabilitation Facilities, "Accreditation Process," webpage, undated-b. As of May 27, 2021: http://www.carf.org/Accreditation/AccreditationProcess/

Committee on the Assessment of Ongoing Efforts in the Treatment of Posttraumatic Stress Disorder, Board on the Health of Select Populations, Institute of Medicine, *Treatment for Posttraumatic Stress Disorder in Military and Veteran Populations: Final Assessment*, Washington, D.C.: National Academies Press, Jun 17, 2014.

Comprehensive Wellness Center, "Intensive Outpatient–IOP–Comprehensive Wellness Centers," webpage, last updated April 24, 2020. As of May 7, 2021: https://www.cwcrecovery.com/treatment-programs/intensive-outpatient-iop/

Council on Accreditation, homepage, undated-a. As of May 26, 2021:
https://coanet.org/

Council on Accreditation, "The COA Accreditation Process," webpage, undated-b. As of April 8, 2021:
https://coanet.org/accreditation-process/

Craske, M. G., Cognitive-Behavioral Therapy, 2nd ed., Theories of Psychotherapy Series, Washington, D.C.: American Psychological Association, 2017.

Craske, M. G., M. B. Stein, G., Sullivan, C. Sherbourne, A. Bystritsky, R. D. Rose, A. J. Lang, S. Welch, L. Campbell-Sills, D. Golinelli, and P. Roy-Byrne, "Disorder-Specific Impact of Coordinated Anxiety Learning and Management Treatment for Anxiety Disorders in Primary Care," *Archives of General Psychiatry*, Vol. 68, No. 4, April 2011, pp. 378–388.

CWC—See Comprehensive Wellness Center.

Defense Health Agency Procedures Manual 6025.13, Vol. 4, "Enclosure 2: Credentialing and Privileging," in *Clinical Quality Management in the Military Health System*, Washington, D.C.: U.S. Department of Defense, August 29, 2019a, pp. 6–42.

Defense Health Agency Procedures Manual 6025.13, Vol. 5, "Enclosure 2: Accreditation and Compliance," in *Clinical Quality Management in the Military Health System*, Washington, D.C.: U.S. Department of Defense, August 29, 2019b, pp. 6–17.

Defense Health Agency, Privacy and Civil Liberties Office, "The Military Command Exception and Disclosing PHI of Armed Forces Personnel," fact sheet, January 5, 2022.

Department of the Air Force Instruction 44-119, *Medical Quality Operations*, Washington, D.C.: Department of the Air Force, September 24, 2007.

Department of the Air Force Instruction 44-102, *Medical Care Management*, Washington, D.C.: Department of the Air Force, January 20, 2012.

Department of the Air Force Instruction 44-121, *Medical: Alcohol and Drug Abuse Prevention and Treatment (ADAPT) Program*, Washington, D.C.: Department of the Air Force, incorporating Change 1, last updated November 21, 2019.

Department of the Air Force Manual 48-123, *Aerospace Medicine: Medical Examinations and Standards*, Washington, D.C.: Department of the Air Force, December 8, 2020.

Department of the Army Regulation 40-502, *Medical Services: Medical Readiness*, Washington, D.C.: U.S. Department of the Army, June 27, 2019. As of May 26, 2021:
https://armypubs.army.mil/epubs/DR_pubs/DR_a/pdf/web/ARN8680_ AR40_502_FINAL_WEB.pdf

Department of the Army Regulation 600-85, *Personnel-General: The Army Substance Abuse Program*, Washington, D.C.: U.S. Department of Defense, last updated August 7, 2020. As of May 26, 2021:
https://armypubs.army.mil/epubs/DR_pubs/DR_a/ARN30190-AR_600-85- 001-WEB-3.pdf

Department of Defense Directive 1350.2, *Department of Defense Military Equal Opportunity (MEO) Program*, Washington, D.C.: U.S. Department of Defense, incorporating Change 2, last updated June 8, 2015.

Department of Defense Directive 6495.01, *Sexual Assault Prevention and Response (SAPR) Program*, Washington, D.C.: U.S. Department of Defense, January 23, 2012.

Department of Defense Financial Management Regulation 7000.14, Vol. 9, Chapter 5, "Temporary Duty Travel (TDY) and Travel Advances," Washington, D.C., last updated January 2022.

Department of Defense Instruction 1010.04, *Problematic Substance Use by DoD Personnel*, May 6, 2020, Washington, D.C.: U.S. Department of Defense, February 20, 2014, updated May 2020.

Department of Defense Instruction 6010.23, *DoD and Department of Veterans Affairs (VA) Health Care Resource Sharing Program*, Washington, D.C.: U.S. Department of Defense, April 3, 2020.

Department of Defense Instruction 6025.5, *Personal Services Contracts (PSCs) for Health Care Providers (HCPs)*, Washington, D.C.: Department of Defense Instruction 6025.18, January 6, 1995.

Department of Defense Instruction 6025.18, *Health Insurance Portability and Accountability Act (HIPAA) Privacy Rule Compliance in DoD Health Care Programs*, Washington, D.C.: U.S. Department of Defense, March 13, 2019.

Department of Defense Instruction 6025.19, *Individual Medical Readiness*, Washington, D.C.: U.S. Department of Defense, May 12, 2020.

Department of Defense Instruction 6490.07, *Deployment-Limiting Medical Conditions for Service Members and DoD Civilian Employees*, Washington, D.C.: U.S. Department of Defense, February 5, 2010.

Department of Defense Instruction 6490.08, *Command Notification Requirements to Dispel Stigma in Providing Mental Health Care to Service Members*, Washington, D.C.: U.S. Department of Defense, August 17, 2011.

Department of Defense Manual 6025.13, *Enclosure 4, Credentials and Clinical Privileges*, Washington, D.C.: U.S. Department of Defense, October 29, 2013, incorporating Change 1, updated July 23, 2020, pp. 21–40.

Department of Defense Safe Helpline, homepage, undated. As of May 27, 2021: https://www.safehelpline.org/

DHA-PM—*See* Defense Health Agency Procedures Manual.

DoD—*See* U.S. Department of Defense.

DoD 7000.14-R—*See* Department of Defense Financial Management Regulation 7000.14.

DoD Manual 6025.13—*See* Department of Defense Manual 6025.13

DoD Safe Helpline—*See* Department of Defense.

Dworkin, Emily R., Suvarna V. Menon, Jonathan Bystrynski, and Nicole E. Allen, "Sexual Assault Victimization and Psychopathology: A Review and Meta-Analysis," *Clinical Psychology Review*, Vol. 56, August 1, 2017, pp. 65–81.

Edwards-Stewart, A., D. J. Smolenski, N. E. Bush, B. A. Cyr, E. H. Beech, N. A. Skopp, and B. E. Belsher, "Posttraumatic Stress Disorder Treatment Dropout Among Military and Veteran Populations: A Systematic Review and Meta-Analysis," *Journal of Traumatic Stress*, Vol. 34, No. 4, August 2021.

Engel, C. C., L. H. Jaycox, M. C. Freed, R. M. Bray, D. Brambilla, D. Zatzick, B. Litz, T. Tanielian, L. A. Novak, M. E. Lane, B. E. Belsher, K. L. Olmsted, D. P. Evatt, R. Vandermaas-Peeler, J. Unützer, and W. J. Katon, "Centrally Assisted Collaborative Telecare for Posttraumatic Stress Disorder and Depression Among Military Personnel Attending Primary Care: A Randomized Clinical Trial," *JAMA Internal Medicine*, Vol. 176, No. 7, July 2016, pp. 948–956.

Foa, Edna B., Elizabeth A. Hembree, and Barbara O. Rothbaum, *Prolonged Exposure Therapy for PTSD: Emotional Processing of Traumatic Experiences: Therapist Guide*, Bethesda, Md.: Oxford University Press, 2007.

Fontana, A., and R. Rosenheck, "Effectiveness and Cost of the Inpatient Treatment of Posttraumatic Stress Disorder: Comparison of Three Models of Treatment," *American Journal of Psychiatry*, Vol. 154, No. 6, June 1997, pp. 758–765.

Forbes, D., G. Hawthorne, P. Elliott., T. McHugh, D. Biddle., M. Creamer, R. W. Novaco, "A Concise Measure of Anger in Combat-Related Posttraumatic Stress Disorder," *Journal of Traumatic Stress*, Vol. 17, No. 3, June 2004, pp. 249–256.

Forbes, D., N. Alkemade, D. Mitchell, J. D. Elhai, T. McHugh, G. Bates, R. W. Novaco, R. Bryant, and V. Lewis, "Utility of the Dimensions of Anger Reactions-5 (DAR-5) Scale as a Brief Anger Measure," *Depression and Anxiety*, Vol. 31, 2014, pp. 166–173.

Fortney, J. C., J. M. Pyne, T. A. Kimbrell, T. J. Hudson, D. E. Robinson, R. Schneider, W. M. Moore, P. J. Custer, K. M. Grubbs, and P. P. Schnurr, "Telemedicine-Based Collaborative Care for Posttraumatic Stress Disorder: A Randomized Clinical Trial," *JAMA Psychiatry*, Vol. 72, No. 1, January 2015, pp. 58–67.

Gong, A. T., S. K. Kamboj, and H. V. Curran, "Post-Traumatic Stress Disorder in Victims of Sexual Assault with Pre-assault Substance Consumption: A Systematic Review," *Frontiers in Psychiatry*, Vol. 10, 2019.

Grant, B. F., T. D. Saha, W. J. Ruan, R. B. Goldstein, S. P. Chou, J. Jung, H. Zhang, S. M. Smith, R. P. Pickering, B. Huang, and D. S. Hasin, "Epidemiology of DSM-5 Drug Use Disorder: Results from the National Epidemiologic Survey on Alcohol and Related Conditions-III," *JAMA Psychiatry*, Vol. 73, No. 1, January 2016, pp. 39–47.

Gray, R., D. Budden-Potts, and F. Bourke, "Reconsolidation of Traumatic Memories for PTSD: A Randomized Controlled Trial of 74 Male Veterans," *Psychotherapy Research*, Vol. 29, No. 5, September 3, 2019, pp. 621–639.

Guina, J., S. R. Rossetter, B. J. DeRhodes, R. W. Nahhas, and R. S. Welton, "Benzodiazepines for PTSD: A Systematic Review and Meta-Analysis," *Journal of Psychiatric Practice*, Vol. 21, No. 4, July 2015, pp. 281–303.

Hallinan, S., M. Gaddy, A. Ghosh, and E. Burgen, "Factor Structure and Measurement Invariance of the Revised Brief Addiction Monitor," *Psychological Assessment*, Vol. 33, No. 3, 2021, pp. 273–278.

Harvey, M. M., S. A. M. Rauch, A. K. Zalta, J. Sornborger, M. H. Pollack, B. O. Rothbaum, L.M. Laifer, and N. M. Simon, "Intensive Treatment Models to Address Posttraumatic Stress Among Post-9/11 Warriors: The Warrior Care Network," *Focus*, Vol. 15, No. 4, 2017, pp. 378–383.

Harvey, Margaret M., Timothy J. Petersen, Julia C. Sager, Nita J. Makhija-Graham, Edward C. Wright, Erika L. Clark, Lauren M. Laifer, Lauren K. Richards, Louis K. Chow, Louisa G. Sylvia, René M. Lento, Laura K. Harward, Joan Clowes, Valerie Brathwaite, Laura K. Lakin, Noah D. Silverberg, Grant L. Iverson, Eric Bui, and Naomi M. Simon, "An Intensive Outpatient Program for Veterans With Posttraumatic Stress Disorder and Traumatic Brain Injury," *Cognitive and Behavioral Practice*, Vol. 26, No. 2, 2019, pp. 323–334.

Health Net Federal Services, homepage, undated. As of May 27, 2021: https://www.hnfs.com/

Health Net Federal Services, *2020 TRICARE West Region Provider Handbook*, Virginia Beach, Va., 2020.

Held, P., B. J. Klassen, R. A. Boley, S. Wiltsey Stirman, D. L. Smith, M. B. Brennan, R. Van Horn, M. H. Pollack, N. S. Karnik, and A. K. Zalta, "Feasibility of a 3-Week Intensive Treatment Program for Service Members and Veterans with PTSD," *Psychological Trauma*, Vol. 12, No. 4, May 2020, pp. 422–430.

Hendriks, L., R. A. de Kleine, T. G. Broekman, G. J. Hendriks, and A. van Minnen, "Intensive Prolonged Exposure Therapy for Chronic PTSD Patients Following Multiple Trauma and Multiple Treatment Attempts," *European Journal of Psychotraumatology*, Vol. 9, 2018, pp. 1–14.

Hepner, Kimberly A., Carol P. Roth, Elizabeth M. Sloss, Susan M. Paddock, Praise O. Iyiewuare, Martha J. Timmer, and Harold Alan Pincus, *Quality of Care for PTSD and Depression in the Military Health System: Final Report*, Santa Monica, Calif.: RAND Corporation, RR-1542-OSD, 2017. As of May 25, 2021:
https://www.rand.org/pubs/research_reports/RR1542.html

Hepner, Kimberly A., Ryan Andrew Brown, Carol P. Roth, Teague Ruder, and Harold Alan Pincus, *Behavioral Health Care in the Military Health System: Access and Quality for Remote Service Members*, Santa Monica, Calif.: RAND Corporation, RR-2788-OSD, 2021. As of May 26, 2021:
https://www.rand.org/pubs/research_reports/RR2788.html

Hilton, Lara G., Salvatore Libretto, Lea Xenakis, Pamela Elfenbaum, Courtney Boyd, Weimin Zhang, and Allison A. Clark, "Evaluation of an Integrative Post-Traumatic Stress Disorder Treatment Program," *Journal of Alternative and Complementary Medicine*, Vol. 25, No. S1, March 2019, pp. S147–S152.

Hoyt, T., and A. Edwards-Stewart, "Examining the Impact of Behavioral Health Encounter Dose and Frequency on Posttraumatic Stress Symptoms Among Active Duty Service Members," *Psychological Trauma*, Vol. 10, No. 6, November 2018, pp. 681–688.

Hoyt, T., D. Barry, S. H. Kwon, C. Capron, N. De Guzman, J. Gilligan, and A. Edwards-Stewart, "Preliminary Evaluation of Treatment Outcomes at a Military Intensive Outpatient Program," *Psychological Services*, Vol. 15, No. 4, November 2018, pp. 510–519.

Hoyt, Tim, and Brianna E. Staley Shumaker, "Disability Status Attenuates Treatment Effects in an Intensive Outpatient Program for PTSD," *Military Medicine*, Vol. 186, Supplement 1, 2021, pp. 190–197.

Humana, "Credentialing of Healthcare Professionals and Facilities," webpage, undated. As of May 27, 2021:
https://www.humana.com/provider/medical-resources/join-humana-network/credentialing-caqh

Humana Military, homepage, undated-a. As of May 27, 2021:
https://www.humanamilitary.com/

Humana Military, "Intensive Outpatient Program (IOP) Provider Certification Application," undated-b. As of May 7, 2021:
https://docushare-web.apps.external.pioneer.humana.com/Marketing/docushare-app?file=3317925

Jaycox, Lisa H., Terry L. Schell, Coreen Farris, Amy Street, Dean Kilpatrick, Andrew R. Morral, and Terri Tanielian, "Chapter Four: Questionnaire Development," in Andrew R. Morral, Kristie L. Gore, and Terry L. Schell, eds., *Sexual Assault and Sexual Harassment in the U.S. Military: Volume 1. Design of the 2014 RAND Military Workplace Study*, Santa Monica, Calif.: RAND Corporation, RR-870/1-OSD, 2014. As of May 25, 2021:
https://www.rand.org/pubs/research_reports/RR870z1.html

Joint Commission, homepage, undated-a. As of May 26, 2021:
https://www.jointcommission.org/

Joint Commission, "Accreditation and Certification," webpage, undated-b. As of April 8, 2021:
https://www.jointcommission.org/accreditation-and-certification/

Joint Commission, "Facts About the Joint Commission," webpage, undated-c. As of April 8, 2021:
https://www.jointcommission.org/about-us/facts-about-the-joint-commission/

Joint Commission, "Why the Joint Commission," webpage, undated-d. As of May 2, 2022:
https://www.jointcommission.org/accreditation-and-certification/why-the-joint-commission/

Kehle-Forbes, S. M., L. A. Meis, M. R. Spoont, and M. A. Polusny, "Treatment Initiation and Dropout from Prolonged Exposure and Cognitive Processing Therapy in a VA Outpatient Clinic," *Psychological Trauma: Theory, Research, Practice, and Policy*, Vol. 8, No. 1, 2016, pp. 107-114. As of May 26, 2021:
https://www.doi.org/10.1037/tra0000065

Kessler, Ronald C., Amanda Sonnega, Evelyn Bromet, Michael Hughes, Christopher B. Nelson, and Naomi Breslau, "Epidemiological Risk Factors for Trauma and PTSD," in R. Yehuda, ed., *Risk Factors for Posttraumatic Stress Disorder*, Washington, D.C.: American Psychiatric Association, 1999, pp. 23–59.

Kilpatrick, D. G., and R. Acierno, "Mental Health Needs of Crime Victims: Epidemiology and Outcomes," *Journal of Traumatic Stress*, Vol. 16, No. 2, April 2003, pp. 119–132.

Kilpatrick, D. G., A. B. Amstadter, H. S. Resnick, and K. J. Ruggiero, "Rape-Related PTSD: Issues and Interventions," *Psychiatric Times*, Vol. 24, June 1, 2007, pp. 50–58.

Kimerling, R., K. Gima, M. W. Smith, A. Street, and S. Frayne, "The Veterans Health Administration and Military Sexual Trauma," *American Journal of Public Health*, Vol. 97, No. 12, December 2007, pp. 2160–2166.

Kip, K. E., and D. M. Diamond, "Clinical, Empirical, and Theoretical Rationale for Selection of Accelerated Resolution Therapy for Treatment of Post-Traumatic Stress Disorder in VA and DoD Facilities," *Military Medicine*, Vol. 183, No. 9–10, September–October 2018, pp. e314–e321.

Knowles, K. A., R. K. Sripada, M. Defever, and S. A. M. Rauch, "Comorbid Mood and Anxiety Disorders and Severity of Posttraumatic Stress Disorder Symptoms in Treatment-Seeking Veterans," *Psychological Trauma: Theory, Research, Practice, and Policy*, Vol. 11, No. 4, 2019, pp. 451–458.

Kroenke, K., T. W. Strine, R. L. Spitzer, J. B. Williams, J. T. Berry, and A. H. Mokdad, "The PHQ-8 as a Measure of Current Depression in the General Population," *Journal of Affective Disorders*, Vol. 114, No.1–3, April 2009, pp. 163–173.

Kroenke, K., R. L. Spitzer, J. B. W. Williams, and B. Lowe, "The Patient Health Questionnaire Somatic, Anxiety, and Depressive Symptom Scales: A Systematic Review," *General Hospital Psychiatry*, Vol. 32, No. 4, 2010, pp. 345–359.

Lande, R. Gregory, Lisa Banks Williams, Jennifer L. Francis, Cynthia Gragnani, and Melanie L. Morin, "Characteristics and Effectiveness of an Intensive Military Outpatient Treatment Program for PTSD," *Journal of Aggression, Maltreatment & Trauma*, Vol. 20, No. 5, July 1, 2011, pp. 530–538.

Landstuhl Regional Medical Center "Evolution Program," webpage, undated. As of May 7, 2021:
https://landstuhl.TRICARE.mil/Health-Services/
Mental-Health-Substance-Abuse/Evolution-Program

Linehan Institute Behavioral Tech, "What Is Dialectical Behavior Therapy (DBT)?" webpage, undated. As of May 26, 2021:
https://behavioraltech.org/resources/faqs/dialectical-behavior-therapy-dbt/

Lorenz, Katherine, and Sarah E. Ullman, "Alcohol and Sexual Assault Victimization: Research Findings and Future Directions," *Aggression and Violent Behavior*, Vol. 31, 2016, pp. 82–94.

Manual of the Medical Department, P-117, "Medical Evaluation Boards," Chapter 18, Washington, D.C.: U.S. Navy, incorporating Change 120, January 10, 2005, pp. 18-1—18-77.

McCauley, Jenna L., Therese Killeen, Daniel F. Gros, Kathleen T. Brady, and Sudie E. Back, "Posttraumatic Stress Disorder and Co-Occurring Substance use Disorders: Advances in Assessment and Treatment," *Clinical Psychology: Science and Practice*, Vol. 19, No. 3, September 1, 2012, pp. 283–304.

Medicare Learning Network, *Inpatient Psychiatric Facility Prospective Payment System*, Washington, D.C.: Department of Health and Human Services, February 2020.

Mendez, Bryan H. P., *FY2021 Budget Request for the Military Health System*, Washington, D.C.: Congressional Research Services, March 2, 2020a.

Mendez, Bryan H. P., *Defense Primer: Military Health System*, Washington, D.C.: Congressional Research Services, No. IF10530, December 14, 2020b.

Meredith, L. S., D. P. Eisenman, B. Han et al., "Impact of Collaborative Care for Underserved Patients with PTSD in Primary Care: A Randomized Controlled Trial," *Journal of General Internal Medicine*, Vol. 31, No. 5, May 2016, pp. 509-517.

Morral, Andrew R., Kristie L. Gore, and Terry L. Schell,, eds., *Sexual Assault and Sexual Harassment in the U.S. Military: Volume 1. Design of the 2014 RAND Military Workplace Study*, Santa Monica, Calif.: RAND Corporation, RR-870/1-OSD, 2014. As of April 22, 2022:
https://www.rand.org/pubs/research_reports/RR870z1.html

Morral, Andrew R., Kristie L. Gore, and Terry L. Schell, eds., *Sexual Assault and Sexual Harassment in the U.S. Military: Volume 2. Estimates for Department of Defense Service Members from the 2014 RAND Military Workplace Study*, Santa Monica, Calif.: RAND Corporation, RR-870/2-1-OSD, 2015. As of June 23, 2022:
https://www.rand.org/pubs/research_reports/RR870z2-1.html

Morral, Andrew R., Miriam Matthews, Matthew Cefalu, Terry L. Schell, and Linda Cottrell, *Effects of Sexual Assault and Sexual Harassment on Separation from the U.S. Military: Findings from the 2014 RAND Military Workplace Study*, Santa Monica, Calif.: RAND Corporation, RR-870/10-OSD, 2021. As of May 26, 2021:
https://www.rand.org/pubs/research_reports/RR870z10.html

Morral, Andrew R., and Terry L. Schell, *Sexual Assault of Sexual Minorities in the U.S. Military*, Santa Monica, Calif: RAND Corporation, RR-A1390-1, 2021. As of April 22, 2022:
https://www.rand.org/pubs/research_reports/RRA1390-1.html

Mott, J. M., M. A. Stanley, R. L. Street, Jr, R. H. Grady, E. J. Teng, "Increasing Engagement in Evidence-Based PTSD Treatment Through Shared Decision-Making: A Pilot Study," *Military Medicine*, Vol. 179, No. 2, February 2014, pp. 143–149.

NASADAD—*See* National Association of State Alcohol and Drug Abuse Directors.

National Association of State Alcohol and Drug Abuse Directors, *State Regulations on Substance Use Disorder Programs and Counselors: An Overview*, December 2012, last updated July 2013.

Nelson Hardiman, "Legal Changes in California Behavioral Health and Addiction Treatment Industries: Key Takeaways," webpage, undated. As of April 22, 2022:
https://www.nelsonhardiman.com/legal-changes-in-california-behavioral-health-and-addiction-treatment-industries-key-takeaways/

Newins, A. R., J. J. Glenn, L. C. Wilson, S. M. Wilson, N. A. Kimbrel, J. C. Beckham, and P. S. Calhoun, "Psychological Outcomes Following Sexual Assault: Differences by Sexual Assault Setting," *Psychological Services*, April 9, 2020.

Nowinski, J., S. Baker, and K. M. Carroll, *Twelve Step Facilitation Therapy Manual: A Clinical Research Guide for Therapists Treating Individuals with Alcohol Abuse and Dependence*, NIAA Project MATCH Monograph Series, Vol. 1, Rockville, Md.: National Institute of Alcohol Abuse and Alcoholism, updated 1999.

Peek, C., *Lexicon for Behavioral Health and Primary Care Integration: Concepts and Definitions Developed by Expert Consensus*, Rockville, Md.: Agency for Healthcare Research and Quality, 2013.

Pietrzak, R. H., R. B. Goldstein, S. M. Southwick, and B. F. Grant, "Prevalence and Axis I Comorbidity of Full and Partial Posttraumatic Stress Disorder in the United States: Results from Wave 2 of the National Epidemiologic Survey on Alcohol and Related Conditions," *Journal of Anxiety Disorders*, Vol. 25, No. 3, April 2011, pp. 456–465.

Posner, K., G. K. Brown, B. Stanley, D. A. Brent, K. V. Yershova, M. A. Oquendo, G. W. Currier, G. A. Melvin, L. Greenhill, S. Shen, and J. J. Mann, "The Columbia-Suicide Severity Rating Scale: Initial Validity and Internal Consistency Findings from Three Multisite Studies with Adolescents and Adults," *American Journal of Psychiatry*, Vol. 168, No. 12, 2011, pp. 1266–1277.

Preston, Samuel L., "Veterans Affairs and Department of Defense Integrated Systems of Mental Health Care" in L. Roberts L. and, C. Warner, eds., *Military and Veteran Mental Health*, New York: Springer, 2018.

Prins, A., M. J. Bovin, D. J. Smolenski, B. P. Marx, R. Kimerling, M. A. Jenkins-Guarnieri, D. G. Kaloupek, P. P. Schnurr, A. P. Kaiser, Y. E. Leyva, and Q. Q. Tiet, "The Primary Care PTSD Screen for DSM-5 (PC-PTSD-5): Development and Evaluation Within a Veteran Primary Care Sample," *Journal of General Internal Medicine*, Vol. 31, No. 10, October 2016, pp. 1206–1211.

Psychology Today, homepage, undated. As of May 27, 2021:
https://www.psychologytoday.com/us

Public Law 115-232, John S. McCain National Defense Authorization Act for Fiscal Year 2019, August 13, 2018.

Ragsdale, K. A., L. E. Watkins, A. M. Sherrill, L. Zwiebach, and B. O. Rothbaum, "Advances in PTSD Treatment Delivery: Evidence Base and Future Directions for Intensive Outpatient Programs," *Current Treatment Options in Psychiatry*, Vol. 7, No. 3, September 1, 2020, pp. 291–300.

RAND Corporation, "RAND Military Workplace Study," webpage, undated. As of April 8, 2021:
https://www.rand.org/nsrd/projects/rmws.html

Rauch, S. A. M., C. W. Yasinski, L. M. Post, T. Jovanovic, S. Norrholm, A. M. Sherrill, V. Michopoulos, J. L. Maples-Keller, K. Black, L. Zwiebach, B. W. Dunlop, L. Loucks, B. Lannert, M. Stojek, L. Watkins, M. Burton, K. Sprang, L. McSweeney, K. Ragsdale, and B. O. Rothbaum, "An Intensive Outpatient Program with Prolonged Exposure for Veterans with Posttraumatic Stress Disorder: Retention, Predictors, and Patterns of Change," *Psychological Services*, Vol. 18, No. 4, November 2021, pp. 606–618.

Reddington, Frances P., and Betsy Wright Kreisel, eds. *Sexual Assault: The Victims, the Perpetrators, and the Criminal Justice System*, Durham, N.C.: Carolina Academic Press, 2017.

Rollison, Julia, Joachim O. Hero, Katie Feistel, Armenda Bialas, Owen Hall, Rosemary Li, Sarah Weilant, Jody Larkin, Coreen Farris, and Kristie L. Gore, *Psychological Harms and Treatment of Sexual Assault and Sexual Harassment in Adults: Systematic and Scoping Reviews to Inform Improved Care for Military Populations*, Santa Monica, Calif.: RAND Corporation, RR-A668-1, forthcoming.

Schnurr, P. P., "Focusing on Trauma-Focused Psychotherapy for Posttraumatic Stress Disorder," *Current Opinion in Psychology*, Vol. 14, April 2017, pp. 56–60.

Schnurr, P. P., M. J. Friedman, T. E. Oxman, A. J. Dietrich, M. W. Smith, B. Shiner, E. Forshay, J. Gui, and V. Thurston, "RESPECT-PTSD: Re-Engineering Systems for the Primary Care Treatment of PTSD, a Randomized Controlled Trial," *Journal of General Internal Medicine*, Vol. 28, No. 1, January 2013, pp. 32–40.

Secretary of the Navy Instruction 5300.28F, *Military Substance Abuse Prevention and Control*, Washington, D.C.: U.S. Department of Defense, Department of the Navy, April 23, 2019.

SECNAVINST—*See* Secretary of the Navy Instruction.

Sherrill, A.M., J. L. Maples-Keller, C. W. Yasinski, L. A. Loucks, B. O. Rothbaum, and S. A. M. Rauch, "Perceived Benefits and Drawbacks of Massed Prolonged Exposure: A Qualitative Thematic Analysis of Reactions from Treatment Completers," *Psychological Trauma*, January 23, 2020.

Skinner, Harvey A., "The Drug Abuse Screening Test," *Addictive Behaviors*, Vol. 7, No. 4, 1982, pp. 363–371.

Sloan, D. M., B. P. Marx, D. J. Lee, and P. A. Resick, "A Brief Exposure-Based Treatment vs. Cognitive Processing Therapy for Posttraumatic Stress Disorder: A Randomized Noninferiority Clinical Trial," *JAMA Psychiatry*, Vol. 75, No. 3, 2018, pp. 233–239.

Spinhoven, P., B. W. Penninx, A. M. van Hemert, M. de Rooij, and B. M. Elzinga, "Comorbidity of PTSD in Anxiety and Depressive Disorders: Prevalence and Shared Risk Factors," *Child Abuse and Neglect*, Vol. 38, No. 8, August 1, 2014, pp. 1320–1330.

Spitzer, R. L., K. Kroenke, J. B. W. Williams, and B. Löwe, "A Brief Measure for Assessing Generalized Anxiety Disorder: The GAD-7," *Archives Internal Medicine*, Vol. 166, No. 10, 2006, pp. 1092–1097.

Stander, Valerie A., Cynthia J. Thomsen, and Robyn M. Highfill-McRoy, "Etiology of Depression Comorbidity in Combat-Related PTSD: A Review of the Literature," *Clinical Psychology Review*, Vol. 34, No. 2, 2014, pp. 87–98.

Steil, R., C. Dittmann, M. Müller-Engelmann, A. Dyer, A.-M. Maasch, and K. Priebe, "Dialectical Behaviour Therapy for Posttraumatic Stress Disorder Related to Childhood Sexual Abuse: A Pilot Study in an Outpatient Treatment Setting," *European Journal of Psychotraumatology*, Vol. 9, No. 1, January 1, 2018.

Tanielian, Terri, and Carrie Farmer, "The US Military Health System: Promoting Readiness and Providing Health Care," *Health Affairs*, Vol. 38, No. 8, 2019.

TheraThink, "Mental Health Reimbursement Rates by Insurance Company [2022]," webpage, undated. As of August 22, 2022: https://therathink.com/reimbursement-rate-comparison/#hard-to-bill

Thielke, S., S. Vannoy, and J. Unützer, "Integrating Mental Health and Primary Care," *Primary Care*, Vol. 34, No. 3, 2007, pp. 571–592.

Thompson-Hollands, J., B. P. Marx, and D. M. Sloan, "Brief novel therapies for PTSD: Written Exposure Therapy," *Current Treatment Options in Psychiatry*, Vol. 6, No. 2, 2019, pp. 99–106.

TRICARE, "Intensive Outpatient Program," webpage, undated-a. As of May 27, 2021: https://TRICARE.mil/CoveredServices/IsItCovered/Intensive-Outpatient-Program

TRICARE, "Military Hospitals & Clinics," webpage, undated-b. As of May 26, 2021: https://www.tricare.mil/Military-Hospitals-and-Clinics

TRICARE, "Find a Doctor," webpage, last updated March 23, 2021a. As of April 22, 2022: https://www.TRICARE.mil/FindDoctor

TRICARE, "Sexual Trauma Intensive Outpatient Program (IOP) Pilot," webpage, February 24, 2021b. As of August 17, 2021:
https://www.tricare-west.com/content/hnfs/home/tw/bene/res/beneficiary_news/dha-launches-pilot-to-tackle-mental-health-effects-of-sexual-tra.html

TRICARE Policy Manual 6010.60-M, Chapter 1, Section 5.1, "Requirements for Documentation of Treatment in Medical Records," incorporating Change 72, updated October 16, 2020.

TRICARE Policy Manual 6010.61-M, Chapter 7, Section 3.5, "Substance Use Disorders (SUDs)–General," incorporating Change 48, last updated June 28, 2019.

TRICARE Policy Manual 6010.60-M, Chapter 7, Section 3.16, "Intensive Outpatient Program (IOP)," incorporating Change 25, updated June 15, 2018.

TRICARE Policy Manual 6010.54-M, Chapter 11, Section 2.1, "Memorandum of Understanding Between the Departments of Veterans Affairs and Department of Defense," August 1, 2002, pp. 3–5.

TRICARE Policy Manual 6010.59-M, Chapter 18, Section 8, "Intensive Outpatient Program (IOP) Pilot To Address Behavioral Health Sequelae of Sexual Trauma," revision C-13, last updated August 28, 2020.

TRICARE Policy Manual 6010.60-M, Chapter 11, Addendum G, "Participation Agreement for Intensive Outpatient Program (IOP) Services," revision C-13, updated November 15, 2017.

TRICARE Policy Manual 6010.60-M, Chapter 11, Section 2.5,"Psychiatric and Substance Use Disorder (SUD) Partial Hospitalization Program (PHP) Standards," change 13, updated November 15, 2017.

TRICARE Policy Manual 6010.60-M, Chapter 11, Section 2.7, "Intensive Outpatient Program (IOP) Standards," change 13, updated November 15, 2017.

TRICARE Policy Manual 6010.60-M, Chapter 11, Section 3.2, "State Licensure and Certification," issued September 20, 1990, change 1, updated March 10, 2017.

TRICARE Reimbursement Manual 6010.61-M, Chapter 7, Section 2, "Partial Hospitalization Program (PHP) and Intensive Outpatient Program (IOP) Reimbursement: Mental Health and Substance Use Disorder (SUD) Treatment," change 10, November 15, 2017.

TRICARE Reimbursement Manual 6010.61-M, Chapter 13, Section 2, "Billing and Coding of Services Under Ambulatory Payment Classifications (APC) Groups," change 21, updated May 30, 2018.

UCF Restores, "TMT Intensive Outpatient Program," webpage, undated. As of May 7, 2021:
https://ucfrestores.com/treatment/tmt-intensive-outpatient-program/

UHS—*See* Universal Health Services.

Universal Health Services, Patriot Support Programs, homepage, undated-a. As of May 27, 2021:
https://patriotsupportprograms.com/

Universal Health Services, Patriot Support Programs, "TRICARE Facilities," webpage, undated-b. As of May 27, 2021:
https://patriotsupportprograms.com/resources/TRICARE-facilities/

Unützer J., M. Schoenbaum, B. G. Druss, and W. J. Katon, "Transforming Mental Health Care at the Interface with General Medicine: Report for the Presidents Commission," *Psychiatry Services*, Vol. 57, No. 1, 2006, pp. 37–47.

Unützer J., H. Harbin, M. Schoenbaum, and B. Druss, "The Collaborative Care Model: An Approach for Integrating Physical and Mental Health Care in Medicaid Health Homes," brief, Center for Health Care Strategies and Mathematica Policy Research, May 2013.

U.S. Army Directive 2020-13, *Disclosure of Protected Health Information to Unit Command Officials*, Washington, D.C., October 26, 2020.

U.S. Code, Title 10, Chapter 47, Uniform Code of Military Justice, Sections 801–940, 1958.

U.S. Code, Title 10, Chapter 47, Uniform Code of Military Justice, Section 920, Article 120, Rape and Sexual Assault Generally, 2017.

U.S. Code, Title 10, Chapter 47, Uniform Code of Military Justice, Section 934, Article 134, General Article, 2016.

U.S. Code, Title 38, Veterans' Benefits, Chapter 17, Section 1720D, Counseling and Treatment for Sexual Trauma.

U.S. Department of Defense, "DoD Travel Allowance Guidance," Appendix B in *Joint Travel Regulations*, Washington, D.C., updated April 1, 2022a, pp. B-1–B-15.

U.S. Department of Defense, "Standard Travel and Transportation Allowances," Chapter 2 in *Joint Travel Regulations*, Washington, D.C., updated April 1, 2022b, pp. 2-1–2-60.

U.S. Department of Defense, "TDY Travel," Chapter 3, Part D, Medical Travel, in *Joint Travel Regulations*, Washington, D.C., updated April 1, 2022c, pp. 3D-1–3-18.

U.S. Department of Veterans Affairs and U.S. Department of Defense, *VA/ DOD Clinical Practice Guideline for the Management of Posttraumatic Stress Disorder and Acute Stress Disorder*, Version 3.0, Washington, D.C., 2017.

VA—*See* U.S. Department of Veterans Affairs.

VA and DoD—*See* U.S. Department of Veterans Affairs and U.S. Department of Defense.

Veterans Health Administration Handbook 1160.01, *Uniform Mental Health Services in Medical Centers and Clinics*, Washington, D.C: U.S. Department of Veterans Affairs, September 11, 2008.

Veterans Health Administration Handbook 1160.04, *VHA Programs for Veterans with Substance Use Disorders (SUD)*, Washington, D.C: U.S. Department of Veterans Affairs, March 7, 2012.

Veterans Health Administration Handbook 1660.04, *Department of Veteran Affairs—Department of Defense Health Care Resources Sharing Agreements*, No. 1, Washington, D.C: U.S. Department of Veterans Affairs, July 29, 2015.

Veterans Health Administration Directive 1660.06, *VA-TRICARE Network Agreements*, Washington, D.C.: U.S. Department of Veterans Affairs, June 28, 2019.

VHA Directive—*See* Veterans Health Administration Directive.

VHA Handbook—*See* Veterans Health Administration.

Walter Reed National Medical Center, "Behavioral Health," webpage, undated. As of May 7, 2021:
https://walterreed.TRICARE.mil/Health-Services/Behavioral-Health

Weathers, Frank W., D. D. Blake, P. P. Schnurr, D. G. Kaloupek, B. P. Marx, and T. M. Keane, "The Clinician-Administered PTSD Scale for DSM-5 (CAPS-5)," U.S. Department of Veterans Affairs, 2013a.

Weathers, Frank W., D. D. Blake, P. P. Schnurr, D. G. Kaloupek, B. P. Marx, and T. M. Keane, "The Life Events Checklist for DSM-5 (LEC-5)," U.S. Department of Veterans Affairs, 2013b.

Weathers, Frank W., B. T. Litz, T. M. Keane, P. A. Palmieri, B. P. Marx, and P. P. Schnurr, "The PTSD Checklist for DSM-5 (PCL-5)," U.S. Department of Veterans Affairs, 2013.

Xu, Y., M. Olfson, L. Villegas, M. Okuda, S. Wang, S. M. Liu, and C. Blanco, "A Characterization of Adult Victims of Sexual Violence: Results from the National Epidemiological Survey for Alcohol and Related Conditions," Psychiatry, Vol. 76, No. 3, Fall 2013, pp. 223–240.

Yasinski, C. M., A. M. Sherrill, J. L. Maples-Keller, S. A. M. Rauch, and B. O. Rothbaum, "Intensive Outpatient Prolonged Exposure for PTSD in Post-9/11 Veterans and Service- Members: Program Structure and Preliminary Outcomes of the Emory Healthcare Veterans Program," *Trauma Psychology News*, January 2018. As of August 22, 2022: http://traumapsychnews.com/2018/01/intensive-outpatient-prolonged-exposure-for-ptsd-in-post-9-11-veterans-and-service-members-program-structure-and-preliminary-outcomes-of-the-emory-healthcare-veterans-program/

Yudko Errol, Olga Lozhkina, and Adriana Fouts, "A Comprehensive Review of the Psychometric Properties of the Drug Abuse Screening Test," *Journal of Substance Abuse Treatment*, Vol. 32, No. 2, 2006, pp. 189–198.

Yudko, E., O. Lozhkina, and A. Fouts, "A Comprehensive Review of the Psychometric Properties of the Drug Abuse Screening Test," *Journal of Substance Abuse Treatment*, Vol. 32, No. 2, March 2007, pp. 189–198.

Zalta, A. K., P. Held, D. L. Smith, B. J. Klassen, A. M. Lofgreen, P. S. Normand, M. B. Brennan, T. S. Rydberg, R. A. Boley, M. H. Pollack, and N. S. Karnik, "Evaluating Patterns and Predictors of Symptom Change During a Three-Week Intensive Outpatient Treatment for Veterans with PTSD," *BMC Psychiatry*, Vol. 18, No. 1, July 27, 2018.

Zatzick, D., G. Jurkovich, F. P. Rivara, J. Russo, A. Wagner, J. Wang, C. Dunn, S. P. Lord, M. Petrie, S. S. O'Connor, and W. Katon, "A Randomized Stepped Care Intervention Trial Targeting Posttraumatic Stress Disorder for Surgically Hospitalized Injury Survivors," *Annals of Surgery*, Vol. 257, No. 3, March 2013, pp. 390–399.

Zatzick, D., S. S. O'Connor, J. Russo, J. Wang, N. Bush, J. Love, R. Peterson, L. Ingraham, D. Darnell, L. Whiteside, and E. Van Eaton, "Technology-Enhanced Stepped Collaborative Care Targeting Posttraumatic Stress Disorder and Comorbidity After Injury: A Randomized Controlled Trial," *Journal of Traumatic Stress*, Vol. 28, No. 5, October 2015, pp. 391–400.